HUEY LONG

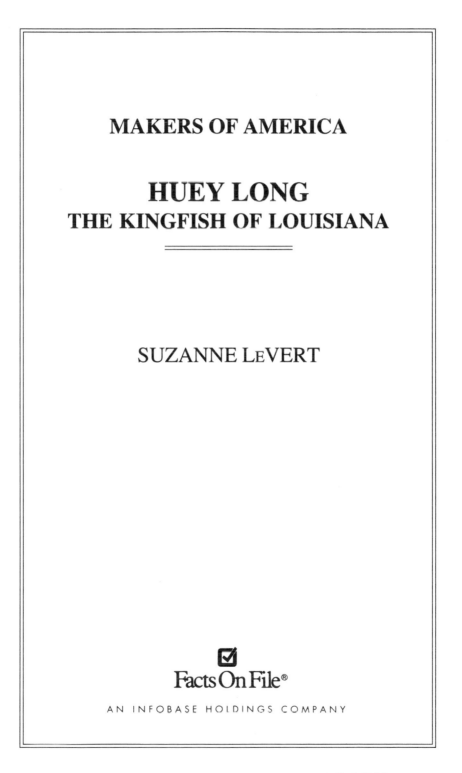

MAKERS OF AMERICA

HUEY LONG
THE KINGFISH OF LOUISIANA

SUZANNE LeVERT

Facts On File®

AN INFOBASE HOLDINGS COMPANY

Huey Long: The Kingfish of Louisiana

Copyright © 1995 by Suzanne LeVert

Facts On File, Inc.
460 Park Avenue South
New York NY 10016

Library of Congress Cataloging-in-Publication Data
LeVert, Suzanne.
    Huey Long : the Kingfish of Louisiana / by Suzanne LeVert.
      p.   cm. — (Makers of America)
    Includes bibliographical references (P.) and index.
    ISBN 0-8160-2880-X
    1. Long, Huey Pierce, 1893–1935. 2. Legislators—United States—Biography. 3. United States. Congress. Senate—Biography.
    4. Governors—Louisiana—Biography. I. Title. II. Series: Makers of America (Facts On File, Inc.)
    E748.L86L48 1995
    976.3′062′092—dc20
    [B]   94-19439

Facts On File books are available at special discounts when purchased in bulk quantities for businesses, associations, institutions or sales promotions. Please call our Special Sales Department in New York at 212/683-2244 or 800/322-8755.

Text design by Debbie Glasserman
Jacket design by Duane Stapp

Printed in the United States of America

RRD FOF 10 9 8 7 6 5 4 3 2 1

This book is printed on acid-free paper.

CONTENTS

PREFACE

T he story of Huey Long—a young man struck down by an assassin's bullet in the prime of his life and at the height of power—is the stuff of which American legends are made. Huey Long is an especially intriguing character, living as he did during one of the most trying times in American history, the Great Depression of the 1930s. Indeed, it can be argued that Huey Long was one of the most influential and imposing figures on the national scene during this political and social crisis.

Almost as interesting to me as Huey Long himself is his home state of Louisiana. Of part-French Canadian extraction, I've long harbored the notion that one of my relatives left Cape Breton Island in the 19th century and made his way to Louisiana, bypassing New England where most of my relatives settled. There is, in fact, a highly speculative rumor that a LeVert sailed with pirate Jean LaFitte to the Barataria Islands in the bayous southwest of New Orleans.

Perhaps because I've lived my whole life in the Northeast, the landscape and culture of Louisiana have seemed as deeply mysterious to me as those of a foreign land: the cypress of the bayous and the lush magnolias that bloom in the spring, the love of good music, food, and conversation. Author Henry Miller once referred to Louisiana as the only state in the Union in which all of the sensual pleasures were given full measure; one only has to visit New Orleans in April to see what he meant.

My goal in writing this biography was to bring to life both Huey Long and his home state, for readers of all ages. I would like to thank Henry T. Nash, a friend and former professor of political science at Wheaton College, and Tony Scott and James Warren, my editors and friends, for helping me fulfill this lifelong ambition. My family and friends, once again, gave me support and fellowship without which I could not have written this book; special thanks go to my parents and to my friend Rebecca Stefoff.

The dedicated help of Virginia Smith, director of the Louisiana Collection at the Louisiana State Library, and her colleague Judy Smith, is also much appreciated. At Louisiana State University's Hill Memorial Library, research librarian Faith Phillips was likewise of special help.

I would also like to thank Dan Fusillier and Mary Ann Weilbacher, who run what must be the most hospitable and gracious guest house—the Josephine—in the city of New Orleans. Their joie de vivre remains an inspiration to me. Most of all, I'd like to thank the dozens of people I spoke with during the weeks I spent in Louisiana. Perhaps more than any other single quality, the people of Louisiana have a marvelous gift for storytelling. Students and cab drivers, real estate agents and physicians—they all generously shared their personal opinions and tales about their home state and its infamous favorite son, Huey Pierce Long.

1

BLOOD ON THE POLISHED FLOOR
The Assassination: September 8–10, 1935

> "I have more enemies in the United States
> than any little man I know of. I am proud
> of my enemies."
> —*Huey P. Long*

Huey Pierce Long, United States senator from Louisiana, arrived in Baton Rouge on the morning of September 8, 1935. The capital city was still caught up in the steamy heat of late summer; before the afternoon was over, the temperature would soar to a sweltering 95 degrees Fahrenheit. Puffy clouds floated across the sky while the sun shone upon the state capitol building, the tallest in the country. Huey Long, as governor, had built the 34-story tower three years before, as much a monument to the extent of his own power, his many foes would say, as to the optimism with which he viewed the future of his home state.

Huey Long arrived in Baton Rouge that Sunday morning to take control of a special session of the state legislature, a session he himself had called for two days earlier. He did so despite warnings by friends and foes alike that his life would be in mortal danger in the state capital. Such rumors prompted Colonel E. P. Roy of the state police to detail 10 policemen to accompany the senator at all times during his visit.

Despite his rise to the national stage as a United States senator, Long held the reins of state power as firmly as he had during his years as governor. His own brother, Julius, a lawyer who helped Huey early in his career, told a reporter in 1933 that "worse political slavery exists in Louisiana today under Huey Long than ever existed anywhere on the North American

1

continent." It was a sentiment echoed by political enemies from within and outside the state.

To his supporters, however, Huey Long was someone who fought for the common man and kept the promises he made no matter what it took. While charges of corruption and dictatorship swirled about him, Long nevertheless maintained unprecedented support among the voters. A factory worker from New Orleans explained Long's appeal this way, "He did more for us poor folks in a day than all the others did in all the years."

Once described as a "bantam rooster type, the kind that could strut sitting down," Huey Long stood 5 feet 11 inches tall and weighed between 160 and 175 pounds, depending upon his dietary habits at the time. His reddish brown hair was cropped short around an expressive, rubbery face, with a bulbous nose and full jowls. He was a man of boundless energy. "Huey came running up" was the start of many a story in Louisiana, in Washington, and wherever he campaigned or lectured across the country. His nickname, handpicked and self-promoted, was the "Kingfish," after a character on the immensely popular radio program "Amos 'n Andy."

After climbing the 48 steps to the entrance of the Baton Rouge capitol, Huey visited the room in which the members of the Ways and Means Committee were considering the 41 pieces of legislation before them. As a United States senator, Long held no official position in the state of Louisiana, but insisted that, as a citizen of the state, he had every right to discuss the bills with the lawmakers. His opinion counted heavily; the Louisiana legislature was known in some circles as the "Longislature."

A few hours later, after committee members had approved all but two of the bills before them, Huey Long retired to his permanent suite, located on the 24th floor of the capitol building. From there, he had a clear view of the city beneath him and of much of the surrounding countryside. It seemed possible, almost, to see the entire state in all its varied landscapes, from the piney hills of the north to the intricate lacework of bayous to the south and west. In the distance lay 65 miles of newly paved highway connecting Baton Rouge to the state's largest city of New Orleans.

That single stretch of highway represented a small percentage of the 2,300 miles of roads constructed since Huey Long had been elected governor in 1928. Promising to take Louisiana "out of the mud," Long's program for change captivated the state's citizens, among the poorest and most isolated in the nation. Their problems, claimed Long, were not of their own making. Instead, men rich with inherited wealth and large corporations motivated by unadulterated greed had raped the state and its people of resources and potential. With a combination of backcountry wit and political calculation, Long spoke to the poor people of Louisiana in their own language, explaining his theories in words and images they could understand. A story he used in speeches and pamphlets depicted an economic problem this way:

> How many men ever went to a barbeque and would let one man take off the table what was intended for nine-tenths of the people to eat? The only way you'll ever be able to feed the balance of the people is to make sure that man come back and bring back some of the grub he ain't got no business with.

Such a crude manner of speaking caused some people to discount him as a "hillbilly and a hick." However, Long rose to power at a time when his message had particular resonance, in Louisiana and throughout the United States. On October 29, 1929, the country and the world were plunged into a deep, long-lasting economic depression. Now, nearly six years later, more than 10 million people—20% of the population—remained unemployed in the United States, and there appeared to be no end in sight to the misery. President Franklin Delano Roosevelt's New Deal program, enacted after he took office in 1933, appeared to have stalled in its efforts to improve the economy. During Roosevelt's term in office, he initiated a dramatic program of relief and reform, which included the establishment of credit agencies to help struggling farmers, and two organizations, the National Recovery Administration (NRA) and the Civilian Conservation Corps (CCC), to boost business and ensure jobs. However, no new federal legislation had been proposed in months and programs already in place were in disarray.

As the effects of the Depression lingered on, more and more people were looking to other leaders for direction, some of whom, like Huey Long, offered radical solutions to the problems facing the country. "One thing, at least, the depression has done for us," the Baton Rouge *Morning Advocate* wrote on January 13, 1930, "it has made it possible for us to mention the word revolution without first pulling down the blinds, peeking under the beds, and giving the maid the day off."

Huey Long brought his revolutionary economic and political theories to the United States Senate in 1932, writing to his supporters that his purpose remained to "break up the swollen fortunes of America and to spread the wealth among all our people . . ." Using the Senate as a base, Long created a new organization, called "Share Our Wealth," and used radio addresses and pamphlets to spread his message to millions of people across the country.

To many economists and political scientists, Long's ideas appeared to be both impractical and unconstitutional. He was charged with being a demagogue, a politician who gains power by arousing people's fears and prejudices and by focusing attention on irrelevant issues. Huey Long's supporters insisted that, as impractical as his plan might be, it pointed to a matter of genuine importance—the distribution of economic resources and power in the United States.

The appeal of Long's ideas, as well as his own dynamic personality, made the "Share Our Wealth" organization a new force in American politics, one whose ultimate power no one

The many faces of Huey Pierce Long, the Kingfish of Louisiana. (Louisiana State Library)

could yet predict. Just a year after he took his seat in Washington, *Time* magazine reported that Long had been one of the top five vote-getters in balloting for "Man of the Year" in 1934.

Long's growing popularity led some people to speculate that he would run for president in 1936. That possibility sparked fear in the highest levels of the Democratic Party and in the Roosevelt administration itself. "We have to remember all the time," President Roosevelt informed an advisor, Rexford G. Tugwell, "that [Long] is really one of the two most dangerous men in the country." The other was General Douglas MacArthur, the chief of staff of the United States Army.

Hoping to diminish Long's power and popularity, President Roosevelt had recently ordered an investigation into Huey Long's taxes and campaign spending practices. The Roosevelt administration had also threatened to reduce the amount of federal aid the state of Louisiana received through New Deal programs.

Long's return to Baton Rouge this September Sunday in 1935 was prompted, in part, by the challenges posed by the Roosevelt administration. One of the bills before the legislature sought to restrict the power of the federal government in Louisiana. It made it a crime—punishable by imprisonment and a fine—for a government agency or officer to exercise any federal power in Louisiana not specifically delegated by the U.S. Constitution. Although his legal assistant, George Wallace, advised him that the bill was unconstitutional, Huey Long had told the Ways and Means Committee on the morning of September 8 that it "simply provides a penalty for violation of Article Ten of the Constitution of the United States." With some hesitation, the committee agreed to put this bill, along with 38 others, before the full House of Representatives for a vote that evening.

As Huey Long waited for the 8:30 P.M. meeting to convene, he met with political allies and friends, including his handpicked successor, Governor O. K. Allen. Through Allen and countless other supporters he had appointed to posts throughout the state, Long remained an almost ubiquitous presence in the Louisiana government. He returned to the capital on a regular basis; the summer of 1935 alone had seen three other such special sessions of the legislature called to order by Long. Despite his new office, he was still called "Governor" in Louisiana.

With single-minded determination, Huey Long steadily increased his power in the state. One bill enacted in the spring gave the governor the power to appoint all election clerks and commissioners, a function once held by locally elected officials. This action prompted one of Long's most ardent foes, representative Mason Spencer, to make an ominous prediction in April 1935:

> When this ugly thing is boiled down in its own juices, it disenfranchises the white people of Louisiana. I am not gifted with second sight . . . but I can see blood on the polished floor of this capitol. For if you ride this thing through, you will travel with the white horse of death.

By claiming that Huey Long was attempting to take the right to vote away from white people, Spencer also confirmed the sorry state of affairs for Louisiana's blacks. Since 1928, the year that Huey Long was elected governor, blacks made up more than 40% of the state's population, yet fewer than 2,000 were on the voting rolls, while more than 367,000 white voters were registered to vote.

Also on the table at this special session of the legislature was another piece of legislation, one that would prove to be Huey Long's ultimate undoing. Through it, he hoped to dislodge an uncooperative enemy, Judge Benjamin Pavy, from a judgeship in the 13th judicial district. Three years before, Pavy had fought against the Long organization during a statewide election and remained one of the only district judges in Louisiana openly hostile to Huey Long. Long now attempted to exact his revenge in two ways: by personal attacks on the judge and by manipulating the political system to render the judge powerless. These were techniques Long had used with much success throughout his career.

Rumors had circulated for several days that Huey Long planned to slander Judge Pavy by resurrecting an old story about the judge's ethnic heritage. Back in 1910, when Benjamin Pavy first ran for office, his opponent claimed that Pavy had African-American blood in him, a charge that in the racist South was considered an insult. Although Huey Long rarely used race as a political issue, he was known to hurl racial epithets in a personal way against anyone who opposed him.

Whether or not Huey Long would have slandered Pavy in this way is still a matter of controversy. However, Long's second line of attack against the judge was well-documented. The bill before this special session of the legislature described a classic case of gerrymandering, redividing election districts in order to gain political advantage. Pavy's district, the 13th, consisted of two parishes: St. Landry, the fourth most populous parish in the state and the most ardently anti-Huey Long, and Evangeline, whose sparse population supported Long.

To Huey Long, the most efficient way of removing Judge Pavy, who had been elected and reelected to his office for 28 years, was by moving St. Landry from the 13th district and placing it in the 15th district. The 15th district consisted of three parishes (districts) that consistently voted for Long and his programs. Judge Pavy would have little chance of winning an election there.

Gerrymandering was considered highly unethical, if not illegal. To his enemies throughout the state, Long's attempt to use this approach to remove a political foe was just one more example of his willingness to use ruthless measures to expand his power. Huey defended himself by claiming that the leaders of St. Landry and Evangeline had themselves requested the redistricting. All he was trying to do was to fulfill the demands of his constituency. "I live and die for my people," he had told his friends in the legislature that morning. The committee obliged the "Governor" by promising to recommend the bill to the full House that night.

At about 8:45 P.M., Huey Long left his apartment and rode the elevator to the first floor. Surrounded by bodyguards, Long made the rounds of committee rooms and chatted with political associates. As he did so, a car pulled up in front of the capitol building. From it emerged a young man 30 years of age, dressed in a white linen suit and wearing dark-rimmed glasses, who then made his way up the steep capitol steps into the great marble lobby.

At 9:20, Huey Long, in a typically rushed fashion, left Governor Allen's office and entered a 10-foot-wide passageway linking the House and Senate chambers. The hallway was crowded with people, many of whom wanted an audience with him. The entourage of plainclothes bodyguards attempted to keep up with the bustling senator but, as Allen's Lieutenant

Governor John Fournet would later recall, "he was a hard man to guard." As Long strode toward one group of men, the man in the white linen suit walked out from behind a pillar and approached Huey.

A drawing made shortly after the Long assassination attempts to re-enact the event that would remain a mystery for decades. (Louisiana State Library)

Suddenly, a shot rang out. Huey Long was heard to cry out once, then was seen stumbling down the corridor. Instantly, his bodyguards turned on the assailant and fired upon him even after he lay motionless on the floor. No one knows for sure how many shots were fired. All told, 30 bullet wounds were found in the front of the body, 29 in the back, and two in the head, but it was impossible to tell how many were caused by the same bullet making an entry and an exit. A journalist at the scene reported that "his back looked like a punchboard with all the numbers out."

In the meantime, Huey Long had disappeared from view. His bodyguards rushed through the corridor, searching for their ward. Finally, an associate, Jimmie O'Connor, found the senator in an isolated stairwell. He grabbed hold of Long and helped him through the back exit and into a car that sped away to Our Lady of the Lake Sanitarium, a hospital located about a quarter-mile away. "I wonder why he shot me," Huey whispered to O'Connor.

Shortly after he arrived at the hospital, as doctors attempted to assess the extent of his injuries, Huey Long was informed of the identity of the gunman: It was Dr. Carl Weiss, a physician practicing in Baton Rouge. He was the son-in-law of Judge Benjamin Pavy, whom Huey Long planned to finagle out of a job and possibly damage with a racist insult. Huey met this information with a shake of his head. "I don't know him," he said of Weiss.

Upon examining Senator Long, Dr. Arthur Vidrine discovered that the bullet, from a .22 caliber pistol, had entered the upper right portion of his abdomen and emerged from the back. Surgery would be necessary to keep the senator from bleeding to death from the damage to internal organs caused by the bullet. Huey requested that Dr. Urban Maes and Dr. Russell Stone, two outstanding surgeons in New Orleans, perform the operation.

Long's assistants contacted Maes and Stone by telephone. The physicians left immediately, by car, for Baton Rouge while Long was prepared for surgery. The senator was fading fast, however. After getting word that the two surgeons had been delayed by a traffic accident, Dr. Vidrine realized that he would have to perform the surgery himself. Vidrine, 39 years of age, owed Huey Long a great deal. He currently held two important positions in the state—dean of the newly created Louisiana State University Medical School and superintendent of Charity Hospital in New Orleans—to which Huey Long had appointed him. His benefactor's life now lay in his hands.

At 12:15 A.M., September 9, the surgery began. Huey Long's immediate family—his wife, Rose, his three children, and his brothers Julius and George—waited for news in a room at the nearby Heidelberg Hotel. Radio announcements alerted the public to the news of the shooting; crowds of concerned supporters and opponents alike gathered outside the hospital and the hotel waiting for news of their fallen Kingfish.

Long's closest political allies remained far closer at hand. Even during surgery, they lined the walls of the operating room and spilled out into the hallways. Fred Dent, one of the political operatives present, recalled, "Here was a man maybe dying and the room was full of politicians." At stake was not merely the life of a man who many of them considered a friend, but also the future of a vast organization that employed thousands of people and disbursed millions of dollars in salaries and services.

The surgery took about two hours to complete. Dr. Vidrine repaired two small wounds in the colon and sutured the abdomen closed. "It all depends on fate," he told Governor Allen when asked about the senator's chances of survival following the operation.

Fate, however, was not on the Kingfish's side. When Maes and Stone finally arrived from New Orleans, they were shocked to discover that Vidrine had failed to perform a simple procedure to test for the presence of blood in the urine during surgery. Such a test would have revealed that the kidney had also been injured by the bullet. This wound continued to bleed, slowly sapping the life out of the senator. Only another operation would save him, and he was not strong enough to withstand the trauma.

All they could do was wait and hope. During the next 24 hours, Huey Long floated in and out of consciousness. When he was awake and alert, he visited with his family, including his aged father who had arrived during the night with Earl Long, Huey's younger brother and frequent political rival. Although initially optimistic, his physicians soon realized how grave the Kingfish's condition had become.

At 11:30 P.M. on Monday night, Seymour Weiss, a close friend and the unofficial treasurer of the Long political organization in Louisiana, announced to the New Orleans *Item*, "We do not expect Senator Long to live through the night. The Senator is sinking rapidly . . ."

At six minutes past four on the morning of September 10, 1935, Huey Long died. Governor O. K. Allen made the official announcement to the press a few hours later. "This marks the death of Huey P. Long," he sobbed, "the passing of the greatest hero for the common right of all people in America." Other commentators were not so kind. "A spectacular figure has been taken from the national scene," a reporter for the Kansas City *Star* wrote. "But his untimely removal cannot be mourned as a national loss." Even in death, Huey Long was a figure of controversy, a man as loved and respected as he was feared and despised.

2

A KINGFISH IS BORN
Early Childhood: 1893–1910

> "My every sympathy has gone out to those
> who toil."
>
> —*Huey P. Long*

As it was on the day Huey Long died in 1935, the United States was in the midst of a deep economic depression on the day he was born—in Winn Parish, Louisiana, on August 30, 1893. Scores of railroads were bankrupt, the steel industry had declined, and about 2.5 million Americans were unemployed. Bank failures for 1893 were the highest yet recorded.

There were many reasons for the economic downturn that started in May with a stock market crash, known as the Panic of '93. Chief among them was the rapid transformation of the nation's economy from one based primarily on agriculture to one in which industry and manufacturing reigned supreme. This transformation, which had begun in earnest during the 1870s and 1880s, caused disruptions in the economy at least once a decade, but the worst by far occurred in 1893. For more than five years, the nation's economy faltered as its economic landscape changed.

In Louisiana, the depression that began the year Huey Long was born made a bad situation worse. Toward the close of the 19th century, Louisiana remained one of the poorest and least industrialized states in the nation; it also had the country's highest illiteracy rate. When cotton and sugar prices plummeted during the panic of '93—the value of agricultural land in the 10 cotton states declined by 31%—the state was further devastated.

12

As would be true again almost 50 years later, this depression fomented political discontent among those most affected by the economic downturn, in this case, the farmers who lived in the South and Midwest. Since the end of the Civil War in 1865, dissatisfaction with their economic and political position had been building steadily among farmers, especially those who owned relatively small plots of land. Not only were crop prices increasingly unstable, but production costs were rising as agriculture became more and more mechanized.

Another important issue for farmers during this period was the growing importance of the railroad in transporting their goods to market. Until 1887, when Congress established the Interstate Commerce Act to regulate railroad rates, the cost of railroad transportation was set arbitrarily by the owners of the railroads themselves, sometimes at rates higher than the small farmer or small businessman could afford.

In addition, and perhaps most importantly, the social status of farmers had declined as the country's economic and cultural life became more centered in the growing cities. Although small farmers never had much economic power, working the land had been considered a noble profession, one that carried with it a certain dignity and respect. Now, with wealth, power, and population concentrated in urban areas, many farmers felt that they were losing even that.

To address these problems, groups of farmers formed a new political organization, called the Farmers' Alliance, in the late 1870s. The Farmers' Alliance began to pressure the federal government to enact policies that would help provide farmers a more stable and equitable standard of living. By 1890, the Farmers' Alliance could claim more than 3 million members throughout the country, the majority of whom lived in the South.

In 1891, members of the Farmers' Alliance joined with factory workers, who also felt powerless in the new industrial economy controlled in large part by big businessmen. Together, the farmers and workers formed a new political party called the People's Party or Populist Party. Populist leaders hoped to create an alliance between all poor and working class people—black and white, rural and urban, Northern and Southern—by showing them that they had more in common with each other than with the political and economic powers-that-be.

In 1892, the Populists nominated James B. Weaver of Iowa for president. Although Weaver lost to Grover Cleveland, he received more than a million popular votes and 22 electoral votes, the most a third party candidate had won in more than 25 years. In addition, nine Populist candidates were elected to Congress, making the Populist Party the most successful third party in American history.

In Louisiana, the Populist movement of the 1890s was centered in Winn Parish, where Huey Long was born and raised. Made up of about 978 square miles in the north-central part of Louisiana, Winn Parish had some important resources, including dense hardwood forests and some land suitable for cotton farming. Unfortunately, most of its rolling surface was covered by thin, infertile soil unsuitable for a plantation economy. As historian Forrest Davis put it, "Winn produced only one crop: dissent."

Winn's population, which numbered just 2,900 when it was incorporated in 1852, was made up largely of farmers who had recently immigrated from other Southern states. Most of Winn's settlers were of English, German, and Scotch background; they were hardworking Protestants. Scattered over a large rural area, isolated from one another as well as from any major city, the citizens of Winn were largely shut out of the mainstream of Southern culture. Most of its residents farmed small plots of land; only about a third of them owned slaves, and those who did, owned only five or six slaves at any given time. (An average working plantation, in comparison, held 15 to 20 slaves.)

Winn Parish first earned a reputation as a center of dissent during the secession crisis of 1860–61 and during the Civil War that followed. To many of Winn's citizens, the conflict between North and South appeared to be "rich man's war and a poor man's fight" from which they had little to gain. For the people of Winn, it was a question not of morality—most of them considered blacks to be inferior to whites and slavery to be a natural state of affairs—but of economics. Indeed, these hardscrabble farmers had little in common with the wealthy planters who were the force behind the coming conflict. Winn's delegate to Louisiana's 1861 secession convention, David Pierson, was one of only seven in the state who refused to sign the ordinance dissolving the bonds of union.

Although Pierson returned home to muster troops for the Confederacy, the parish's loyalty to the Southern cause continued to wane as the war dragged on; along with neighboring Jackson Parish, it was the state's most notorious center for draft avoidance and desertion. Indeed, up to half of Winn's able-bodied young white men may have hidden in the parish's dense forests—"joining up with General Green" as the practice became known—rather than be conscripted into the Southern army.

Among those who avoided service in the Confederacy was Huey Long's grandfather, John Murphy Long, who first arrived in Winn Parish on the day before Christmas, 1859. Born and raised in Springfield, Ohio, John harbored strong nationalist sentiments. His father, James Long, was a Methodist from Baltimore, Maryland, where the Long family could trace their heritage to before the American Revolution. "[John] was a Yankee," his third son and the father of Huey Long, later recalled. "He was with the North during the war, but he stayed here and kept his mouth shut."

John Long, a tall man with blond hair and blue eyes, settled with his family on a small plot of land about 30 miles south of the parish seat of Winnfield. He and his wife, Mary Wingate of Mississippi, eventually had 14 children together. Their third eldest son, Huey Pierce Long Sr., would become the patriarch of one of Louisiana's most powerful political families.

Like most of their neighbors, the Longs were farmers. Huey Sr. and his brothers and sisters worked long hours helping their father to raise cattle and harvest subsistence crops of corn, celery, and other vegetables. Although Huey had a keen intelligence and harbored a desire to become a physician, it fell to him to help his father hold the family farm together. When John became too ill to manage the farm himself, Huey took over and soon discovered that he not only enjoyed farming, he was also good at it. Slowly but surely, he increased his family's economic standing in the community.

In 1875, at the age of 23, Huey felt established enough to marry Caledonia Tison, a 15-year-old girl from Winn Parish. The two made a handsome pair. Old Hu, as Huey Sr. soon became known to his friends and neighbors, was six feet tall, with golden brown hair and deep brown eyes. He had a boisterous personality and a booming voice; the Longs' caretaker,

Jesse Roberts, recalled, "You always knew two blocks before you got there that he was there."

With coal-black hair, hazel eyes, and a petite figure, Old Hu's wife Caledonia looked like the Southern lady she was brought up to be. Unlike the Longs, the Tisons had been a family of some standing in Winn Parish for several decades before the Civil War; they owned a number of slaves and educated their children better than most families of the time. Caledonia would instill in all her children a love of literature and of learning.

In their first home, located on John Long's farm, Old Hu and Caledonia had four children: Charlotte, Julius, a daughter named Helen who died in infancy, and George. As his family continued to grow, and his financial situation to improve, Old Hu bought 320 acres of land in Winnfield. He moved Caledonia and the children to a large, log house located on the property in 1886. It was in this house that three more Long children were born—two girls, Olive and Clara, and on August 30, 1893, a boy named Huey Pierce Long Jr.

"Every time I hear about that cabin," Huey Long's sister Charlotte (known as Lottie) would later complain, "it gets smaller and smaller." Indeed, her brother Huey, Louisiana's future governor and senator, would "warp things for political reasons" during his campaigns. He often described his first home as a tiny log cabin and his childhood as consisting of endless days of manual labor. By doing so, he hoped to win the hearts and votes of the struggling farmers he considered his core constituency. He may well have done so, but he also incurred the wrath of his siblings. "He made us all so mad," admitted Lottie.

The truth was that Huey Long was born in a drafty but otherwise comfortable four-room log house, complete with a twelve-foot-wide hallway that ran through the center of the dwelling. Moreover, he lived in the log house for no more than a year, at which time Old Hu again moved his family into improved circumstances. Huey's younger brother Earl and two sisters, Caledonia and Lucille, were born in a smaller, but better built saltbox house located on the same property. The Longs lived in this home for about 12 years.

From an early age, Huey's remarkable energy and intelligence were apparent to his family and neighbors. "Huey was nervous, curious about everything," recalled his older brother

Julius. "Our father used to say that he'd jump in the well to see what it was like if it wasn't kept covered. He wouldn't stay still." Huey learned to walk at just nine months and, if left to his own devices, the little boy would toddle to the front gate of the yard, unlatch it, and sit by the side of the road to watch the world go by. Huey's older sister, Olive, was assigned the difficult task of keeping her red-headed little brother out of trouble. "Run, Ollie, run," her mother would yell, "he's done it again."

Despite his future claims to hard work in the fields—"Rising before the sun," Huey wrote in his autobiography, "we toiled until dark"—Huey's farm chores were probably fairly limited. His father recalled that "Huey may have plowed a little, but not much," while his sister, Lottie, was more blunt: "Huey and Earl never got near a plow unless somebody else was using it." Huey admitted that he hated farm work, but claimed that his experience with it gave him sympathy for the hardworking men and women whose livelihoods depended on it.

Huey despised going to school almost as much as he did performing manual labor. A frequent sight in the neighborhood was that of Caledonia hauling her young boy to school with the aid of a peachtree switch. Although no record exists of his earliest school years, companions remember him as "an active boy, mentally and physically active." His grades, however, were not good, especially in "deportment"; Huey could not keep still in class and constantly interrupted his teachers.

There were at least two reasons for Huey's problems at school. One was that the boy had a profound distaste for rules and regulations of any kind, especially those that kept him from doing exactly what he pleased. Whenever possible, Huey simply broke the rules that disturbed him. When the Winnfield school system added a grade level to its high school, Huey found a way to avoid adding that year to his own education. Instead of joining with his other classmates for the seventh grade, Huey presented himself for admission to the eighth grade. His impudence paid off; after a short quiz in several subjects, the eighth grade teacher agreed to promote him.

His precocious intelligence was another reason for Huey's difficulties at school; he was, more than likely, simply bored. Schools throughout Louisiana were notoriously under-supplied and poorly staffed; a state publication of the time referred to schools as "sloughs of contented ignorance." By the time

Huey entered the eighth grade, Winnfield's high school was located in a new, three-story brick building, but most towns in the area were not so well-endowed. A schoolteacher, brought to teach in a nearby, northeastern Louisiana town, described the dreadful conditions in her journal:

> Most of the houses in the far-flung community were of logs, but the school, like some of the cheaper places, was a boarded-up, ceilingless shack with wide cracks in the walls. The school's furniture was homemade, desks were two long tables with tops that sloped to a peak at the center. The benches were backless.

A fundamental problem in the schools as well as in the community at large was the scarcity of books. In fact, neither the school nor the town of Winnfield had a library; except for textbooks that were usually handed down from sibling to sibling for several years, books were difficult to procure. Fortunately, the Long family had its own supply of books, most of them collected during Caledonia's childhood.

Huey was an avid reader from an early age. The macabre stories of Edgar Allan Poe, the poetry and drama of Shakespeare, and the novels of Dickens were among the collection from which Huey could choose. What Huey loved best, however, were true stories of great leaders who rose to power against all odds; his two favorite books were a history of the world by John Clark Ridpath, which focused on the exploits of such leaders, and a biography of Napoleon, the brilliant and egomaniacal general who created an empire in late-18th-century France. Huey was also exposed to current events through the *Saturday Evening Post* magazine and the Atlanta *Constitution* newspaper, to which his parents subscribed.

The most often read book in the Long home was the Bible. Both Old Hu and Caledonia were devoted Baptists, and religion played an important role in Huey Long's upbringing. The First Baptist Church of Winnfield saw the Longs at every service, including Sunday school, Wednesday night prayer meeting, and revivals. Until Huey left home at the age of 16, he was a regular attendant at all religious ceremonies. "We went to every funeral within ten miles," he later wrote. For a short time in his youth, Huey even considered becoming a minister.

In 1901, when Huey was about eight years old, the once tranquil and isolated community of Winnfield began to undergo a fundamental change. The Arkansas Southern railroad extended its line through the town, bringing with it new people, new money, and new priorities. Once a town with "a kindly philosophy of 'live and let live,'" as Huey later put it, Winnfield was transformed into a community "yielding to commercial enticements."

It was at the tender age of eight years that Huey witnessed his first farm foreclosure, in which the local bank sold to the highest bidder the property of a family who could not afford to pay its mortgage. This event, which deprived a needy family of a home and allowed a wealthier man to reap the benefits, made a lasting impression on the sensitive boy. "I was horrified," he later wrote, "I could not understand. It seemed criminal."

At the same time, the arrival of the railroad and subsequent infusion of capital helped the Long family to prosper. Old Hu, then 47, began selling portions of his 320-acre farm as residential lots for Winnfield's expanding population. With the profits, he invested in more land on the outskirts of town, thereby becoming one of the town's largest landowners and most adept real estate agents. In 1907, when Huey was about 13 years old, the Long family moved into a graceful, two-story, ten room colonial-style house. It was one of the most impressive in Winnfield.

In addition to attending to his business interests, Old Hu dabbled in local politics. Perhaps because of his relative wealth and high standing in the community, Hu never aligned himself with the more radical elements active in the area. In 1901, at the height of Populist Party influence in Winn, Hu ran for state senate on the Democratic ticket. His platform, however, had a distinctly Populist message; a local newspaper, the Colfax *Chronicle,* described Hugh as a "stock raiser, frugal and industrious, who is opposed to corporate control of the government . . . and is a firm believer in a better school system." His son Huey would latch onto those same issues during his own campaigns several years later.

As a youth and an adolescent, Huey inevitably heard much talk about the inequitable distribution of wealth, and the exploitation of people by railroads, banks, and other corporations. When Huey was a teenager, his Winn neighbors elected several Socialists to local offices and in 1912 gave the Socialist presidential candidate, Eugene Debs, 36% of their votes, the highest percentage in the state. Harley Bozeman, a lifelong resident of the parish and friend of Huey Long, described his home town as "a hotbed of feuding and fussing and Huey was raised right in the middle of it."

Huey's father explained the town's influence on his son to a reporter in 1947:

> There wants to be a revolution, I tell you. I seen this domination of capital; seen it for seventy years. What do these rich folks care for the poor man? They care nothing— not for his pain, nor his sickness, or his death. Why their women didn't even comb their own hair. They'd sooner speak to a nigger than a poor white. They tried to pass a law that only them as owned land could vote. And when the war come, the man that owned ten slaves didn't have to fight. . . . Maybe you're surprised to hear talk like that. Well, it was just such talk that my boy was raised under, and that I was raised under.

Before politics became his own passion, Huey tried his hand at a few other occupations. At the age of 13, he learned to set type and worked after school for the *Baptist Monthly Guardian,* a newsletter of the denomination published in Winnfield. When his skill at typesetting improved, he was employed part-time by the *Southern Sentinel,* a local newspaper to which he contributed an occasional article.

Huey's career in journalism lasted only about a year, until a peddler passing through town offered him and his friend, Harley Bozeman, a supply of books to sell on their own. The two 14-year-old boys attacked the job with enthusiasm. Huey hired a horse and wagon and stormed the countryside; when his door-to-door technique failed, he and Harley stood on street corners and auctioned them off to the highest bidder.

Although the boys never made much money from the venture, they were allowed to read the remainders. Huey's favorite book from this batch was *The Count of Monte Cristo,* which he read several times throughout his life. He later told a friend one reason why he loved this book so much: "That man in that book knew how to hate and until you learn how to hate you'll never get anywhere in this world."

Huey's first experience in politics came to him through his older brother, Julius. In 1908, when Huey was not quite 15, Julius, an attorney 14 years older than Huey, was involved in a campaign for a candidate running for Congress. Julius' candidate, Theodore Wilkinson, was running an uphill race against the leading candidate, Jared Y. Sanders, in the Democratic primary. Julius entrusted his younger brother to campaign in a polling precinct in Winnfield. On election night, Huey's powers of persuasion were evident; although Wilkinson lost statewide, he won by 300 votes in Huey's precinct. "All I remember," Huey later admitted, "is that the first time I knew anything [about politics], I was in it."

Huey's political education continued when he joined his high school's debate team in 11th grade. Through his experience on the team, he learned to master his already considerable talents as a speaker. "I can't remember back to a time when my mouth wasn't open whenever there was a chance to make a speech," he later told a reporter. He and Harley Bozeman were chosen to represent Winnfield at the annual state high school rally at Baton Rouge. At the rally, students from all over the state competed in a series of events, including a debate and a declamation (speech-making) competition. The event took place on the campus of Louisiana State University.

Huey stayed with T. H. Harris, the state superintendent of education for more than 30 years, for the duration of the rally. Harris wrote of his first meeting with Huey Long in his memoirs:

> The boy was a perfect portrait of the man to follow. He came swaggering into the house, leaving the baggage for others to bring in, and introduced himself to Mrs. Harris . . . He was always late for meals, left his clothes all over the bathroom floor, and had everybody in the house awake by five or six in the morning.

Although he had diligently practiced his speech for weeks, Huey lost his event, for which he read an oration written by Henry W. Grady, a progressive politician from Georgia. Despite a rule barring a student from entering more than one contest, Huey then demanded that he be allowed to participate in the debate, the subject of which was "Should women be given the vote?" His impromptu speech, in which he declared that he was against women's suffrage because "they got too many rights right now and that's why no boy ain't gonna win nothing here," in front of the debate chairman won him third place in the competition and a scholarship to Louisiana State University.

Once again, his brashness had served him well. His self-confidence was evident in the goodbyes he made to the Harrises: "Mrs. Harris, you have been mighty good to me and when I get to be Governor, United States Senator, and President of the United States, I am going to do something for you. I am on my way and will not be stopped by a committee of ignorant professors."

Unfortunately, Huey was indeed stopped, at least momentarily, by school administrators. Shortly after returning from the debate in Baton Rouge, Huey was either expelled from high school or decided to quit on his own. Apparently, he had infuriated the school's principal by distributing a petition calling for his resignation. The reason for Huey's protest was that, once again, Winnfield added an extra grade level to its high school. Huey's 11th grade class would have to attend another year of classes in order to graduate.

Huey's decision to leave school was also influenced by another fact: Despite the scholarship to Louisiana State University, he would not be able to afford to attend because he lacked the money for living expenses and school supplies. Frustrated, Huey decided to strike out on his own.

One month shy of his 17th birthday, Huey Long left home for good when his old friend, Harley Bozeman, offered him a job as a salesman. Huey jumped at the chance to escape Winn Parish and see some of the world around him. He left the day after he received Bozeman's offer, packing a few belongings in a shoebox and jumping on the train that would take him to Shreveport, a small city about 60 miles northwest of Winnfield. As Bozeman himself put it, Huey was "away ahead of everybody in knowing how to trade and traffic," and for the next four years, he would prove his ability on the road in his home state and throughout much of the South.

3

ON THE ROAD IN LOUISIANA
Long Explores Louisiana: 1910–1915

> "I can sell anything to anybody."
> —*Huey P. Long*

With a starting salary of $19 a week, Huey Long launched into his first full-time job as a door-to-door salesman with customary enthusiasm. Using his considerable powers of persuasion, he charmed housewives and storekeepers into buying his product, a cooking oil made from processed cottonseed called Cottolene. Within just a few days, he accumulated more orders than any other junior salesman in the history of the company.

His boss, Victor Thorsson of the N. K. Fairbanks Company of New Orleans, thought that Long's "gift of gab" and memorable personality were the qualities that made him so successful. In addition to these assets, however, Long developed sales techniques to help him get ahead. He used posters and circulars to advertise Cottolene and provided potential customers recipes that used the cottonseed oil to the best effect. If all else failed, Huey would set about cooking a meal for the entire family. He rarely left a home without making a sale.

By buggy, by train, and on foot, Long traveled in northern Louisiana during the summer and fall of 1910. He met hundreds of farmers and merchants, wealthy and poor, in small cities and tiny villages. Talking to them with a unique combination of country wit and slick salesmanship, he made an indelible impression on the people he met; very few who came into contact with the fast-talking salesman would ever forget him.

Huey Long left Winnfield for the first time at the age of 17. He would spend about four years on the road as a traveling salesman. (Louisiana State Library)

In addition to gaining experience and earning money, Long's job with Cottolene brought him another reward: a woman to love and, eventually, to marry. In September 1910, Long organized a baking contest to promote Cottolene in the city of Shreveport. One of the contestants was a petite, black-haired woman named Rose McConnell, who entered a white cake made with sugar, flour, egg whites, vanilla, milk, and two-thirds of a cup of Cottolene. Huey Long was impressed, not only with the cake but with the woman who claimed to have baked it. (Huey's sisters would insist forever after that Rose had no talent as a cook; "Her mother baked that cake," insisted Lottie.) After a little gentle prodding from Huey, Rose agreed to date him.

Rose McConnell was "the most beautiful woman" Huey Long had ever met. A stenographer and secretary for a local insurance company, Rose was organized, efficient, and independent. In many ways, it was an attraction of opposites: Where Huey was excitable and impetuous, Rose had a quiet, demure way about her. Older than Huey by about 16 months, Rose seemed infinitely more mature and stable than her suitor.

In fact, Rose was reluctant to become involved with this brash young man, a 17-year-old boy with more than his share of self-confidence but without a high school diploma, financial resources, or a secure future. She knew that being a salesman would not hold his interest for very long, nor would the life of an average man ever be enough for him. Instead he seemed obsessed with politics. He wrote scores of letters to senators and congressmen in Washington about political issues. "I want to let them know I'm here. I'm going to be there someday myself," he told her. "It almost gave you the cold chills to hear him tell about it," Rose admitted later. "He was measuring it all." Nevertheless, there was something alluring about Huey Long. Although it would be two and half years before she would agree to marry him, romance between them quickly blossomed.

It soon appeared that Rose had good reason to worry about Huey Long's future. Despite their continued success, he and Harley Bozeman were fired from the N. K. Fairbanks Company a week before Thanksgiving in 1910. Their dismissals had little to do with their abilities; the company had financial problems that forced it to cut back on expenses by closing the northern Louisiana sales office. In addition to forcing him out of a job, this experience showed Huey how powerless the average worker could be in the face of a large corporation.

Huey Long returned home to Winnfield, discouraged and unsure of what his next step should be. His older brother, Julius, encouraged him to obtain his high school diploma and head for law school, promising him a partnership in his own law firm. Huey's resolve to graduate from high school lasted only until school administrators informed him that he lacked the credits necessary to graduate in one semester; he would have to return in the fall. As usual, when confronted with a rule that held him back, he simply ignored it and took matters into his own hands. He decided to drop all classes except those that met in the morning and find himself a job.

A few months later, Harley Bozeman, now a salesman for the Houston Packing Company, found his friend working as a stenographer in a Shreveport plumbing company. Huey jumped at Bozeman's offer to return to the road as a salesman, this time selling cured meats, lard, and canned goods to wholesale distributors. Long's first assignment for the Houston Packing Company took him to the Texas state capital of Austin in January 1911.

After once again proving his abilities as a first-rate salesman, Huey was sent to open a new sales office in Little Rock, Arkansas. From there, he would supervise a sales team that would cover all of west Tennessee, north Mississippi, and parts of Alabama. For his services, he was paid a salary of about $25 per week plus expenses. Over the next few months, Huey spent several days each week on the road. In addition to soliciting orders from wholesale distributors, Long indulged his interest in politics by attending political rallies and demonstrations whenever possible.

He found he had ample opportunities to do so. Fifty-five years after the close of the Civil War, the South now struggled to regain the political and economic power it had lost with its defeat. From the still scarred countryside, there emerged a number of political leaders who fed on Southerners' fears, prejudices, and longings for respect and dignity. These leaders were called "demagogues," a term that later would be applied to Huey Long himself.

The word *demagogue* is derived from the Greek *demos agogos,* a leader of the people. Euripedes, the Greek philosopher and dramatist, referred to a demagogue as "a man of loose tongue, intemperate, trusting to tumult, leading the populace to mischief with empty words." His definition could certainly be applied to the men Huey Long now saw on his journeys throughout the South.

In Arkansas, he became acquainted with one of the region's most colorful political characters, Senator Jeff Davis, also known as the "Wild Ass of the Ozarks" and the "Karl Marx of the Hill Billies." Known for his fiery speeches and flamboyant personal style, Davis often used racist rhetoric to stir up support among white voters. More importantly, however, he appealed to all farmers who resented the fact that the focus of power was shifting away from rural communities toward urban, and mostly northern, areas. He was not afraid to refer to his constituents as "hillbillies" and "rednecks"; in fact, he invoked these monikers as terms worthy of respect. Huey Long would never forget either the style or the substance of Davis's message.

Long was also deeply impressed by another Southern leader, James K. Vardamann of Mississippi. Former governor of the state, Vardamann launched a campaign for the United States Senate in 1911 during which Huey saw and heard "the Great White Chief" over the course of the spring and summer. Wearing an immaculate white linen suit, white boots, and a black Stetson hat, Vardamann appeared as a savior to the poor white farmers who felt ignored by the reigning forces in the state and in Washington. Huey noticed that Vardamann was not afraid to criticize his opponents in a very personal and vindictive way. In one speech, he called one of his critics, "a degenerate by birth, a carpet bagger by inheritance, a liar by instinct, a slanderer and assassin of character by practice, and a coward by nature." The crowd around him roared its approval.

Long's political education was furthered by witnessing the campaigns of Vardamann's protege, Theodore Bilbo, also called "the Man" by his constituents. Like his mentor, Bilbo was known to use slander and invective against his opponents. He dressed in suits outfitted with red suspenders and wore red ties as a symbol of his appeal to the "rednecks" of the South. When asked about his attire by a reporter, he responded that he wore "suspenders to keep up my pants and the tie to keep up my courage."

Huey Long learned a great deal from these men, not only about the Southern white mentality of the time, but also how to appeal to it by stressing personal style over political substance. He also noticed that they were able to make promises to their constituents that they could not and did not keep and yet appeared not to suffer for it at the polls. Jeff Davis, for example, served three terms as state attorney general and two terms as United States senator without affecting any significant changes in the lifestyle or economic power of Arkansas' poor white population.

After working out of Little Rock for several months, Long was transferred to Memphis, Tennessee. He rented rooms in one of the finest hotels in the city and lived comfortably. Unfortunately, a drought in the spring caused cotton prices to plummet and thus the entire Southern economy to suffer, making it difficult for Long to maintain his high sales figures. He received a letter terminating his employment in late August. A few weeks of unemployment later, Huey Long was completely broke, sleeping on park benches. Huey wrote in his autobiography, "I spent money as I made it," a habit that unfortunately would last a lifetime.

Once again, he turned to his family for advice and assistance. His mother, harboring hopes that Huey would become a minister, arranged for him to attend Oklahoma Baptist University. Huey's older brother George, a practicing dentist in Norman, Oklahoma, offered to pay some of Huey's expenses and sent him money for transportation. After just a few months at the university, however, Huey decided that he belonged in law school. Probably lying about his educational background, he enrolled at the University of Oklahoma, again accepting monetary assistance from George. He also secured a job working for the Dawson Produce Company as a salesman.

For one semester, Long attempted to apply himself to his studies. In his autobiography, *Every Man a King,* he described the months he spent at the law school as "the happiest days" of his life and claimed that he attended classes regularly and managed to earn about $100 a month selling produce to grocery stores. What he didn't admit was that he also enjoyed drinking and gambling, activities that left him broke and with barely average grades—three C's and an incomplete—at the end of the semester.

Although a political race kept Huey involved in a campaign during the summer, he soon grew bored with Oklahoma and decided not to return to the university in the fall. Once again, his old friend Harley Bozeman was able to secure him a job. The Faultless Starch Company of Kansas City hired Huey Long as a sales manager and sent him to its regional office in Memphis, Tennessee. Huey had one goal—to make a lot of money—and he was able to do just that for several months. Earning $125 a month, plus expenses, Huey could afford to return to his favorite suite at the Gayosa Hotel. He brought his younger brother, Earl, into the business and together with several other salesmen, they worked the Memphis area with great success.

With his current circumstances so favorable, Huey decided that the time was right to press his suit with Rose. She had resisted his proposals of marriage for more than two years, but he now hoped to convince her of his financial security and commitment to her. During the Christmas holiday, he traveled to Shreveport to spend time with the woman he longed to marry.

Back in Memphis after the holidays, however, Huey fell into a pattern of drinking and gambling that troubled Rose and other members of his family. Finally, Rose agreed to marry her persistent suitor, probably more to calm Long down than because she felt ready to do so. They were married on April 12, 1913, by a Baptist minister in the lobby of the Gayosa Hotel. Typically, Huey Long found himself short of cash at a crucial time; Rose paid the $11 marriage license fee out of her own pocket.

The couple moved to a small, comfortable apartment and, for several months, Huey's life seemed to be stable and on track. But in October, he was hit with two brutal blows: First, his mother, Caledonia, died of influenza at the age of 52. Then, a few weeks later, he learned that he had lost his third job in as many years when the Faultless Starch Company reduced its sales force. Huey and Rose returned to Winnfield to live at the Long family home.

Fortunately, Long quickly found another position. As a salesman for the Chattanooga Medicine Company, he sold a variety of bogus concoctions, including the Wine of Cardui, which was supposed to "stimulate the blood," and a laxative called Black

Rose McConnell was the "most beautiful" girl Huey had ever seen. The couple were married in 1913. (Louisiana State Library)

Draught. Long's territory included large portions of his home state, allowing him to explore the bayous of the south and west as well as the region's largest city of New Orleans for the first time.

Indeed, as Huey Long traveled across his home state as a salesman, he saw that there were at least three Louisianas to visit—the north, the south, and the city of New Orleans—each with its own unmistakable flavor. His own home region, the piney hill country of the north, was populated by the Anglo-Americans of Irish, German, and Scottish ancestry. Protestants or Baptists, they believed in hard work, the Bible and, often, abstention from liquor and other worldly pleasures. The whites of the north, who made up more than 60% of the population, tended to be quite racist in their attitudes, perhaps because most of the blacks who lived among them were their former slaves.

Since the turn of the century, the north had become the center of oil and timber production. Although these resources produced a welcome economic boon, they also brought with them a host of ecological and political problems; both oil and timber companies were largely controlled by out-of-state corporations that cared little for the long-term survival of the land or its inhabitants. Huey Long, himself born and raised in the north, knew its people and their challenges well.

He came face-to-face with an altogether different culture, however, when he traveled through southern Louisiana. This region of the state was populated largely by Catholics of French or Spanish descent who were known to be far more tolerant and easy-going than their northern compatriots. The racial composition here was just the opposite from that of the north: Blacks made up about 60% of the population and many of them had lived as free men and women since their arrival in Louisiana. Although racism certainly existed in the south, it was less ferocious and violent than in the north.

Between the "hard-shelled Baptist country" of the north and the "soft-shelled crab land" of the south lay the city of New Orleans, in spirit if not in strict geographical terms. If anything united the two distinct rural regions of Louisiana, it was a profound mistrust—some would say dislike—of the state's largest city and its inhabitants, whom the farmers tended to think of as wealthy, arrogant, and insensitive to the needs of the rest of the state.

From its founding as the colony's capital in 1718, New Orleans thrived as one of the New World's premier ports because of its strategic site at the mouth of the Mississippi River. It attracted merchants and businessmen of all nationalities anxious to make a profit on a variety of imported and exported goods, including cotton and other agricultural products and, until well into the 19th century, slaves. It was also known for its passionate devotion to the sensual pleasures, including fine food and music, as well as to the vices of gambling, prostitution, and drinking.

New Orleans had developed a strict social caste system that remained in full force when Huey arrived to sell his wares in the summer of 1914. At the top of the social scale were the Creoles, descendants of the colonials of French or Spanish ancestry, and the Anglo-Americans who arrived later and were of British ancestry. The Creoles, who fiercely guarded their status as the city's original founders, lived in the Vieux Carré, also called the French Quarter. The Americans, on the other hand, moved Uptown, where they built elegant mansions in the Garden District. In the city's less desirable areas and at the other end of the social ladder, were the blacks, the Irish, and other more recent immigrants.

Huey Long, now 21 years old, had spent almost four years as a traveling salesman. During this period, he had met thousands of people throughout his home state; in fact, he once stated that he "knocked on every door in every town of more than 400 people" in Louisiana. He wrote the names and addresses of people he admired, who admired him, or who had made an enemy of him on index cards; he filed many others in his remarkable memory.

Talking with his customers and potential customers, Huey began to understand what issues were of most importance to them. Like Vardamann, Bilbo, and Davis, he learned how to communicate with all of the poor people of his state, the Cajuns and blacks of the south as well as the rednecks of northern Louisiana with whom he had grown up, urban dwellers as well as farmers and fishermen.

As rewarding as his experience as a salesman had been, Huey Long knew it was time to pursue his real dream of becoming a politician—and that meant buckling down to study law. Despite his relative success in business, he remained without resources and again had to turn to a family member for help.

This time, his eldest brother, Julius, provided Huey with the necessary funds. If Rose would accompany Huey, and thus provide a stabilizing influence on the often erratic young man,

Julius would give his younger brother $50 a month for nine months to cover his expenses at Tulane Law School in New Orleans. Huey also managed to borrow about $250 from a friend in Winnfield, S. J. Harper, who would prove to be helpful to Huey later in the young man's career as well.

Long departed for New Orleans immediately to arrange his coursework and obtain an apartment in New Orleans. When Rose joined him a week or two later, she knew why Julius felt that her presence was necessary: Huey had rented a large apartment on Prytania Street, in the city's elegant Garden District, for $35 a month, well over half their entire monthly budget. She quickly moved them to a small studio on Carrollton Street, closer to the ivy-covered buildings of Tulane University and much less demanding on their budget.

Because Long had yet to receive his high school diploma, he was forced to enroll in law school as a special student. As such, he could audit classes, then take an exam that would admit him to the Louisiana bar. For once, Huey applied himself fully to the task at hand. After a full day of classes, he studied for many hours every day, often working into the early morning. He constantly quizzed his professors, inside and outside the class. "The bell would ring," a fellow student observed, "and he'd always have one more question to ask."

In the spring, Huey Long realized that Julius' endowment would soon be depleted. Although the course of study usually took three years, Huey decided he was ready to be examined in just one. Once again, Long ignored rules he found inconvenient. Instead of being examined in the parish in which he would practice, as Louisiana law required, he simply presented himself to the board that met in New Orleans. Instead of waiting for the regular bar exam to take place in June, he convinced the chief justice of the state Supreme Court that he deserved a special oral exam given by a panel of attorneys. He impressed the panel, as much with his quick wit and extraordinary memory as with his grasp of the law, and was admitted to the Louisiana bar on May 15, 1915 at the age of 21.

Almost immediately, he and Rose left for Winnfield where Huey had agreed to join his brother Julius' law firm as a partner. Huey Long, however, never lost sight of his ultimate goal of becoming a politician. He later admitted, "I came out of that courtroom running for office."

4

A TASTE FOR POLITICS
Attorney-at-Law and Railroad Commissioner:
1915–1924

> "Huey Long don't take out after topwaters
> but after the big fish."
>
> —*Huey P. Long*

A s a young boy, Huey Long had amused some of his classmates, and offended others, by adding to his name a title usually reserved for full-fledged attorneys or elected officials; even books he owned in the second or third grade were inscribed "The Honorable Huey P. Long" or simply "Hon. Huey P. Long." His self-confidence—some would say arrogance—was fully intact upon his homecoming to Winnfield in the summer of 1915, but he also had a law degree to validate his once precocious designation. After he and Rose moved into the family homestead, Huey began to practice law with his brother Julius.

Fourteen years Huey's senior, Julius was taller, thinner, and had a far more thoughtful and dignified manner about him than his often impetuous younger brother. Julius had long acted as Huey's adviser and mentor, recognizing Huey's potential for greatness perhaps better than anyone else in the family. Now a district attorney for Winn Parish, Julius was, at least at first, happy that Huey agreed to join him in his established law firm.

Within three months, however, the Long brothers parted company after bitter arguments made it impossible for them to work together. Julius claimed that Huey insisted upon defending the very criminals Julius was prosecuting for the state and that his brother would shamelessly steal clients from him whenever business was slow. Huey, on the other hand, claimed that Julius did not treat him with the respect he deserved as a full partner in the firm. They also argued incessantly about money.

The altercation was not the first argument Huey had had with one of his siblings, nor would it be the last. Even as a child, claimed Julius, Huey was "always disagreeable among his brothers and sisters," perhaps because of his strong need to be the center of attention at all times. It was a trait that would continue to annoy members of the Long family throughout their lives.

Of his six siblings, Huey was closest by far to two of his brothers, Julius and Earl. With them, he formed the strongest bonds of affection and had the most ferocious of fights. Many of their battles, which would involve political as well as personal matters, often were fought in full view of an increasingly fascinated public. "Other families," noted one Winn resident, "did not talk about their feuds even though they might be killing each other. The Longs advertised theirs."

After his argument with Julius in the fall of 1915, Huey decided to open his own law office. He rented space in the Bank of Winnfield from his Uncle George, the bank president, for $4 a month. Pleading poverty, he managed to have the first month's rent deferred for several weeks. With help from Rose, Huey furnished the 8-by-10 foot space with a table, two chairs, an old typewriter he purchased on credit, and an incomplete set of law books. He proudly hung out a sign that read "Huey P. Long, Lawyer" and waited for clients to retain him.

Unfortunately for the fledgling lawyer, business was slow. There were several other, more experienced attorneys already practicing in Winnfield and only so many residents needing the advice of counsel. To help make ends meet, Huey became the Winnfield correspondent for a Shreveport newspaper, writing articles about local events and issues. More than a few of his pieces involved a sharp young attorney named Huey P. Long, whose name was slowly but surely becoming known to the people of northern Louisiana.

As he had done so often in the past when short of money, Huey also took to the road as a traveling salesman. Leaving Rose to manage the office and keep him informed of new business, Huey sold a variety of consumer goods for the Never Fail Company of Greenfield, Ohio. He did well enough to warrant an advance from the company to buy his first automobile, a Model T Ford, in which he carried his wares and toured the countryside. The first car to be mass-produced, the Model T sold for $500, which allowed average working men, men like Huey Long, to enjoy the fruits of the Industrial Revolution as never before.

As usual, Huey gained far more than a salary from his job as a salesman. He took the opportunity to meet new people and reintroduce himself to the hundreds of others he had met on previous trips. He also learned firsthand how treacherous the roads of Louisiana were, even for those lucky enough to own an automobile. Little more than dirt paths, Louisiana roads had long been the bane of the state's residents. When it rained, the paths became impassable rivers of mud fraught with invisible potholes that frequently caught the wheels of a car, or horses' hooves. Indeed, Huey soon learned to carry a bottle of whisky to offer as a reward to farmers who helped him dig his car out of a ditch.

Back in Winnfield, his law business began to grow and take more and more of his attention. For a time, Long took on cases that no one else in the community wanted, primarily divorces between black couples. Eventually, however, he began to handle a relatively new field of law: that of workmen's compensation. In 1914, the state legislature passed a law, called the Employers Liability Act, that allowed men who had been injured on the job to be compensated for their medical expenses and the wages they lost while they recuperated. For the first time, corporations could be held accountable for their workers' health and safety, and Huey Long was there to make sure they lived up to their responsibilities.

Although these cases earned Long little money—in fact, he was nearly evicted when he couldn't pay the office rent—they helped him formulate a theme that would define his political philosophy and career for ever afterward. From this time forward, Huey Long would present himself as someone who would fight for the little man against the big corporation, the poor man against the rich, the helpless against the powerful.

Long's first major case pitted him against the very bank from which he rented office space and for which his Uncle George served as president. An elderly woman known in Winnfield as the Widow DeLoach claimed that an official of the bank had embezzled money from her account. Although the official later returned some of the funds and gave her an I.O.U. for the rest, he had since left Winnfield and was nowhere to be found. The bank claimed that it was not liable for the $275 still owed to Widow DeLoach since she had accepted the official's personal I.O.U.

In a larger city, such a case probably would not have attracted much attention. In Winnfield, however, the sight of a feisty young lawyer defending the rights of a "poor widow woman" against a cold, heartless financial institution drew dozens of fascinated citizens to the courtroom. Once inside, they were treated to a display of Long's oratory and showmanship. He made sure that the widow brought her children, dressed in little more than rags, into the courtroom "for the jury to see." He harangued the bank's executive officers for denying the widow and her children money that was clearly owed to them.

By the end of the trial, public sentiment against the bank ran high throughout Winnfield. When the jury returned a verdict in favor of the Widow DeLoach, Huey's reputation as a lawyer grew by leaps and bounds. "I cleaned hell out of them in that suit," he later recalled, "and after that I had all the law business I could handle."

Although the practice of law now took up much of his time, Long's political ambition was not forgotten. In May 1916, he joined forces with a friend, state senator S. J. Harper, in bringing a series of amendments to the state legislature in Baton Rouge. Known as the Harper Amendments, these pieces of legislation were meant to bolster the Employers Liability Act of 1914 by providing more liberal damages to injured workers who won cases against their employers. Such new laws would certainly benefit Huey Long, who took a percentage of the damages awarded to his clients as his fee for bringing the cases forward.

It was the first time that Long had seen the legislature in action and he found the "formalities, mannerisms, kow-towing and easily discernible insincerities" to be "disgusting." When he appeared to speak before the committee as a concerned citizen, he was refused the floor. When he again arose, the chairman of the committee asked him whom he represented. "Several thousand common laborers," Huey answered. "Are they paying you?" asked the chairman. "No," Huey replied. "Well, they seem to have good sense," the chairman snapped, provoking laughter from his fellow committee members.

Huey Long, however, refused to be silenced. In his characteristically forceful voice, he challenged the entire committee's ethics. "For twenty years," he lectured, "has the Louisiana Legislature been dominated by the henchmen and attorneys of the interests. Those seeking reforms have from necessity bowed their heads in regret and shame when witnessing the victories of these corrupting influences at this capitol."

Outraged by the 22-year-old attorney's audacity, the committee immediately and unanimously voted down the amendments. At first glance, it would seem that Huey Long had gone too far, losing his case with deliberately inflammatory words. In fact, he went to Baton Rouge knowing that few of the amendments had any chance of passing into law. It was the opportunity to make his name and his opinions known in the halls of the Louisiana State Capitol that brought him to the committee room that day.

His plan appeared to work. Word of Huey Long's appearance before the legislature and his shocking, but clearly heartfelt, accusations spread across the state. The powers-that-be in Louisiana, particularly wealthy "interests" who had been accused of colluding with legislators, began to take note of the young upstart from Winnfield; indeed, the list of men who considered Huey Long a potentially dangerous political enemy grew daily.

At the same time, the people to whom Long most appealed— the poor and middle-class workers and farmers who felt left behind and cheated by the wealthy and powerful—flocked to his office. One case, involving a land dispute between the Wheelus family of north Louisiana and the Urania Lumber Company, earned Huey more than $1,500 worth of richly timbered land when he won the case for the family. Excited by his success, he impetuously donated $150 to a nearby church in search of donations.

By 1917, Huey Long was an established figure in north Louisiana, with a growing law practice and a reputation as a fiery speaker with strong opinions about the way the state should be run. He was also a family man, with a wife and one daughter, born in April 1917 and named Rose for her mother. When the United States entered World War I in that same month, Huey chose to stay at home and tend to his family and career. Before the war was over, Rose and Huey would have a second child, Russell B., born in November 1918.

World War I, a bloody struggle for territory and economic superiority among the great powers of Europe, raged for nearly three years before the United States sent men to fight alongside Britain, France, and Russia. Considered a fight for democracy and justice against the imperialistic aspirations of Germany, Austria-Hungary, and Turkey, World War I aroused passionate sentiments among Americans. Willingness to fight in the war became synonymous with loyalty and patriotism; those who chose not to fight for religious, moral, or political reasons were labeled traitors and, frequently, imprisoned.

Huey Long's decision not to join the army, therefore, had the potential to cause him great political and social harm. When his opponents called him a coward and a disloyal American, which they did throughout his career, he defended himself by saying, "I did not go because I wasn't mad at nobody over there." More likely, he simply wanted to take advantage of the prestige and attention he was receiving to further his career. In any case, he sought and won a deferment on the grounds that he was the sole support of his wife, child, and aged father.

Huey's loyalty was called into question again when he defended his friend and colleague United States Senator S. J. Harper. In February 1918, Harper was charged with violating the Espionage Act by speaking out against United States involvement in the war. According to Harper, World War I was not being fought to protect democracy but rather to line the coffers of bankers and war profiteers. Harper published a pamphlet entitled *The Issues of the Day—Free Speech—Financial Slavery,* which called for a "conscription of wealth": If the nation insisted upon drafting young men to fight, it should force the wealthy to finance the war with their large fortunes.

Because popular support of the war was intense in Louisiana and throughout the country, very little dissent was tolerated. A federal grand jury in Alexandria indicted Harper, claiming that his words amounted to obstructing the draft, a crime under the Espionage Act. Huey Long rushed to Harper's defense, despite the fact that his cause was unpopular; "Harper was my one good friend in Winnfield," Huey explained.

Huey, who worked with his brother Julius on this case, used his usual combination of trickery and bombast. His trickery began even before the trial was in full swing. After the jury pool was named, Huey identified those he felt would be hostile to his case. Knowing that they were being watched by federal officials, he slyly offered to buy them drinks or dinner; although he never discussed the case with them, they were disqualified when prosecutors learned that they had become friendly with the opposition.

Huey's oratory was not as successful, however. Several times during the course of the trial, the judge reprimanded the young lawyer, at one point threatening him with jail for contempt of court. He also incensed the judge by issuing a press release denouncing the indictment as political persecution. By the end of the trial, Huey and the judge were on such poor terms that Huey asked Julius to give the closing arguments. Thanks to the efforts of both Long brothers, Harper was acquitted on all counts on March 19, 1918.

The Harper case represented another milestone in Long's career. In addition to responding to the bonds of friendship and taking advantage of the chance to put himself in the public spotlight, Huey had agreed to help Harper because he largely concurred with his thinking—about the war and about the meaning of wealth in this country. Ever since he witnessed a farm foreclosure at the age of eight, Huey Long was acutely aware of the power the rich had over the lives of the poor. Despite the risks to his professional life and his political aspirations, Huey Long supported a cause in which he deeply believed.

During the course of the trial, Long wrote a letter to the New Orleans *Item* that summarized an article that had impressed him in the *Saturday Evening Post*. He repeatedly cited statistics, which were taken from a report issued by President Woodrow Wilson's Industrial Relations Commission:

> A conservative estimate is that about sixty-five or seventy percent of the entire wealth of the United States is owned by two percent of the people. Sixty-eight percent of the whole people living in the United States own but two

percent of its wealth . . . Authorities on education tell us that eighty out of every one hundred people in the United States never enter high school; only fourteen out of every thousand get a college education . . . What do you think of such a game of life, so brutally and cruelly unfair, with the dice so loaded that the child of today must enter it with only fourteen chances out of a thousand in his favor of getting a college education?

As his social philosophy began to mature, Huey Long grew anxious to begin the career he had dreamed about all his life—politics. Unfortunately, he was too young to run for the office he most aspired to attain: Louisiana required its governor to be at least 30 years old. For a time, Huey considered running for district attorney against his brother Julius, but Harley Bozeman convinced him that the competition might break the frequently tenuous bonds of family once and for all. Instead, Huey should make a run for a little known but potentially powerful position on the Railroad Commission.

The three-member Railroad Commission had been created by the 1898 Louisiana constitution to regulate the practices and rates of railroads, steamboats, and other vessels; subsequent legislation expanded its duties to include overseeing telephone and telegraph companies. The commission also had a measure of control over oil pipelines, although the law was less clear on that point. Despite its inherent power, the commission had not been very active and its members were all traditional Louisiana politicians who tended to sympathize with the very corporations they were elected to regulate.

In 1918, Burk A. Bridges was running for reelection to the Railroad Commission in the Third District, which comprised north Louisiana's 28 parishes. A wealthy conservative from Claiborne Parish, Bridges had every reason to believe he would easily win a second six-year term. That was before Huey P. Long entered the race and began a 20-year political career that would transform the face of Louisiana forever.

Indeed, Long's campaign for Railroad Commissioner was unlike any seen before in north Louisiana. As was true for most of Louisiana's political offices, the election of a Railroad Commissioner took place in two stages: First, a primary election was held among all candidates in the race. Then, if no candidate won more than 50% of the vote, a run-off election between the two top voter-getters was held several weeks later. Bridges, Long, and three other candidates began to prepare for the September primary early in 1918.

Determined to win a post he considered a stepping stone to the governor's office, Long tapped all his resources for the race. Remembering the lessons he had learned from political showmen like James K. Vardamann and Theodore Bilbo, Long decked himself out in a bright white linen suit (donated by S. J. Harper) and drove from campaign stop to campaign stop in a shiny automobile. "Hell," Huey later exclaimed to a reporter, "they told me I'd have to drive around in an old buggy with a horse, and wear slouchy clothes and chew tobacco. But not me . . . I wanted them to think I was something, and they did."

Traveling to nearly every town and village in north Louisiana, Huey Long campaigned day and night. He gave speeches in town squares, in neighborhood parks, and at backyard barbecues. Late at night, he often stopped at a farmhouse, woke up its residents, and introduced himself as the leading candidate for Railroad Commissioner. If they seemed hospitable, he might ask to spend the night, offering them a dollar or two for their troubles. Rather than be offended by such behavior, the farmers and their families were impressed with a man who worked long into the the night. Most of these people had never laid eyes on Long's opponents or any other politician, for that matter. Huey Long made them feel important.

In addition to his own remarkable energy and stamina, Huey Long also called upon his family and friends as resources. Julius, perhaps relieved that he would not be facing Huey in a race for district attorney, served as his brother's campaign manager; Earl paid the filing fee of $125 and campaigned door to door; and Rose mailed out hundreds of envelopes stuffed with her husband's campaign literature. Other family members and supporters hung posters and campaign circulars on tree trunks, fence posts, and walls of buildings throughout the Third District. When funds ran low, Huey turned to friends for contributions. Winn Parish's assessor, Oscar K. Allen, known to his friends as O. K., borrowed $500 from a local bank and donated it to the campaign. Huey Long never forgot the favor; Allen would play a large role later in Huey's career.

The Long campaign reached thousands of north Louisiana citizens during the summer of 1918. The message these people heard would become a familiar one in the coming years: Huey Long was a common man who would fight for the rights of all common men. Huey Long was not like the other politicians who were serving the interests of big business and ignoring the needs of average citizens. Huey Long would work hard to supply the poor, struggling people of Louisiana with the basic necessities of life, and more.

If elected Railroad Commissioner, Long promised to force the railroads to extend their lines and services—a burning issue in the isolated backwoods of northern Louisiana—and the utility companies to reduce their rates. He also attacked his opponent without mercy, calling 54-year-old Bridges an "old man" and a "pawn of the special interests."

Long's campaign style and message convinced enough people to vote for him that he placed a close second to the incumbent in the September primary, beating out the three other candidates. Several weeks of hard-hitting campaigning later, Long managed to poll just 635 more votes than Bridges in the runoff. As would be true in every election in which he participated, Long's major source of support was the rural areas of his district; generally speaking, the smaller the town, the more votes he amassed. In fact, Long carried only four of the 28 parish seats. Nevertheless, at the age of 25, Huey Long had won his first political victory.

Following the election, Long moved his family and his law practice from Winnfield to Shreveport. Located about 70 miles northwest of Long's hometown, Shreveport was Louisiana's second largest city after New Orleans and the center of the state's burgeoning oil business. The fastest-growing industry in Louisiana, the oil business offered a clever and resourceful lawyer like Huey Long myriad opportunities for advancement in income and visibility.

As he had in Winnfield, Long brought forward many cases involving workers injured on the job who sought compensation from their employees. In addition, he began to work on behalf of small, independent oil companies, also known as "wildcatters." Through helping the independents, Huey acquired stock in several small oil companies in lieu of cash payments for his services; he enhanced his holdings by purchasing additional stock himself.

During this period, the independents were struggling to hold their own against increasingly powerful oil corporations like Gulf Oil, Texas Oil and, particularly, Standard Oil. Standard Oil, a corporation with headquarters in New Jersey, was the biggest purchaser, carrier, and refiner of oil in Louisiana. Not only did Standard have the capital to purchase more land and drill more wells than wildcatters, but it also owned almost all of the pipelines used to transport oil throughout the state, thus controlling a crucial facet of the oil business in Louisiana. Its profits, however, were largely returned to New Jersey because Louisiana had little power to tax out-of-state corporations.

Louisiana, one of the poorest states in the nation, was therefore denied an important source of revenue, revenue that could have been used to fund the building of roads, the improvement of schools and other public works projects. The effort to force corporations like Standard Oil to pay their fair share of taxes to the state from which they derived so much profit would form the cornerstone of Huey Long's political career.

In early 1919, a case arose that involved Huey Long both as a Railroad Commissioner and a stockholder in three independent oil companies. These three companies owned part of the Pine Island oil wells, located about 15 miles north of Shreveport. During World War I, the United States government required large quantities of Pine Island crude to use as diesel oil in military tanks and aircraft. The crude was first purchased from the independents by larger oil companies, including Standard Oil, and then resold to the government.

Unfortunately for investors, however, the crude from Pine Island was unsuitable for use as kerosene or gasoline. When the war ended and the need for diesel fuel dramatically decreased, the market for the product nearly disappeared. Standard Oil told the independents that it would no longer buy any crude from the Pine Island wells. Furthermore, Standard claimed it would also refuse to transport Pine Island oil through its pipelines. Long and other Pipe Island investors were ruined just "because the three pipeline companies said so," as Huey wrote in his autobiography.

Because the Railroad Commission's charter was vague on the question of pipeline regulation, it was unable to take action against the corporation. However, if Standard Oil and the other pipeline companies were considered public utilities rather than private corporations, Long postulated, they would fall clearly under the commission's jurisdiction. With the grudging support of his fellow commission members, Long urged Governor Ruffin Pleasant to call a special session of the Louisiana state legislature. The purpose of the session: to declare Standard Oil a public utility.

Standard Oil appeared to win the day when Governor Pleasant refused to consider Long's motion. For Huey Long, however, the fight had just begun. For the rest of his political career, Huey would fight to control Standard Oil in Louisiana. In addition, he would use Standard as a symbol to represent all big business, declaring the corporation to be the ultimate enemy of poor and working people everywhere. According to Huey Long, the interests and needs of both individuals and the state of Louisiana were sacrificed in order to satisfy the greed of corporate profitmakers like John D. Rockefeller and his wealthy corporate cohorts.

Furthermore, Long insisted that a primary responsibility of government was to protect the people from such potential corporate abuse. Both corporations and wealthy individuals should be forced to pay a higher share of taxes and thus contribute more to the health and welfare of the vast majority of citizens. Any politician or government official who did not share this opinion, according to Long, was a pawn of the special interests and thus an enemy of the people.

Without doubt Huey Long had more than altruistic motives for espousing these ideas. He was well aware that by attacking the biggest and most powerful entities in the state he had a chance to attract the votes of the majority of citizens, the very poor and working people he claimed government should protect. Journalist Thomas A. Harris, who closely followed Huey Long's career, wrote that Huey "recognized at once the political value of a successful fight against the Standard. Suppressing him was like trying to empty the Mississippi River with a dipper."

During the next several years, Huey Long juggled his responsibilities as Railroad Commissioner and lawyer, all the while keeping his eyes focused on Louisiana's political scene. "My occupation is multifarious," Huey wrote to his brother George in 1919, "law, railroad commissioner, politics, oil—which in general leaves me in a deranged mental state at the end of each week." Indeed, although Long's energy seemed boundless, it would take its toll. He was known to overindulge in alcohol on occasion and frequently suffered from insomnia. "Three o'clock in the morning is the same as three in the day to me," Huey was heard to comment. These bad habits did not appear to affect his work, however, and he constantly impressed others with his stamina. Harry Gamble, an acquaintance from Winnfield, recalled wondering how "anybody born in this semi-tropical climate could have so much energy."

Long took advantage of every available opportunity to make himself better known throughout his state. In 1919, the Democratic Party held a rally in Hot Wells, a health spa in Rapides Parish in central Louisiana. The purpose of the meeting was to kick off the 1920 gubernatorial race by introducing the candidates. Although Long was still too young to run for the office, he arranged to speak to the crowd near the end of the meeting. Using typical inflammatory language, he called the present governor, Ruffin Pleasant, "the criminal who disgraces the gubernatorial chair" for having refused to stand up to Standard Oil by calling a special session. He harangued Standard Oil as well, describing the company as a "highway bandit."

The next day, the newspapers were full of accounts describing Long's remarks. Most were negative: "vicious" was how the Alexandria *Town Talk* described the speech. Others were impressed with both the content and the speaker. The New Orleans *States* reporter noted that "Mr. Long took the audience into his confidence. 'I haven't got a dime, but I'm not afraid for my political future and I don't care whether I've got any or not.'" Huey's "candid" comments were fundamentally untrue—he was financially quite comfortable and had an insatiable craving for political power—but they served his purpose by attracting people who were looking for a courageous reformer.

In the 1920 gubernatorial race, Huey threw his support behind John M. Parker, another man considered to be a reformer. Parker, who lost a previous bid for governor in 1916, was one of the wealthiest men in the state. The picture of a Southern gentleman, Parker had a frequently sunburned face, black hair shot with grey, and piercing brown eyes. "When he looked at you," wrote reporter William Wiegand, "you felt that he was looking into your soul."

Although Parker ran a profitable business buying and selling cotton in New Orleans and owned a plantation in Baton Rouge, he was not a traditional conservative. Instead, he joined the Progressive Party in 1912 and ran on its platform in 1916, both for governor of Louisiana and as vice-president on the party's national ticket. After losing both bids, he rejoined the Democratic Party but continued to press for increased funding for education and roads, increased taxes on corporations, and other progressive measures.

Huey Long supported Parker in 1920, mainly because he thought Parker was hostile to large oil interests and would regulate pipelines more effectively. Huey campaigned hard, contributing more than $2,000 of his own money to print and deliver circulars in support of Parker. He also gave speeches in the most remote areas of the state, nearly one every day for two and a half months, outlining what he thought Parker's pipeline bill promised to be. For his part, Parker was pleased to have Huey's backing because he needed more support from voters in north Louisiana.

Their relationship would soon sour. Parker won the Democratic primary in January 1920 by more than 11,000 votes, then went on to win an overwhelming victory over his Republican opponent later in the spring. Not long after, Huey found reason to break with his former ally. Rather than further polarize the state's business and political interests, Parker offered to compromise on the pipeline bill and invited Standard Oil representatives to help write the legislation. He further disappointed Huey Long and others when he failed to include a progressive income tax and an oil severance tax as part of the new state constitution, enacted in 1921. The severance tax, a tax on resources taken or "severed" from the land, like oil or timber, was particularly controversial, as it would fall most heavily on large corporations like Standard Oil.

Parker's actions caused Long to become one of the governor's most vociferous political enemies. In a circular he distributed to every legislator in the state, he charged that the Standard Oil lobby was "about to make itself a part of the legislative machinery of Louisiana." In another tract, he wrote that Parker had traded in "offices which belong to the people and bartered them away in a manner becoming an ancient ruler of a Turkish domain." Huey typed and photocopied these and other circulars in his office at the Public Service Commission, a stronger agency created by the 1921 constitution to replace the Railroad Commission.

Long was relentless in his attacks, so relentless that Governor Parker decided to sue the contentious young lawyer for libel. The governor was supported by a host of politicians and big-business representatives who hoped that a libel conviction would force Huey to resign his office as Public Service Commissioner and ruin his future public career as well.

Huey stood his ground and, with brother Julius serving as his counsel, defended his right to speak out against the governor. He claimed that because none of his remarks were made against the governor personally, the libel charge was spurious. "I ain't interested in saving Governor Parker's personal soul," he testified before the court in Baton Rouge, "I've been trying to do something for the state."

The people of Louisiana were transfixed by the trial, which involved the governor, a Public Service Commissioner, and several other officials. On November 8, Judge Brunot declared Huey Long guilty of libeling Governor Parker. He sentenced Huey to 30 days in the parish prison, but suspended the penalty, then fined him $1 or, alternatively, asked him to serve one hour in prison. The sentence was so mild, the judge explained, because Huey was guilty of libel only in a technical sense. "Yours is an impulsive nature, given to ill-considered and at times indiscreet utterances," Brunot said to Long. It was a statement with which no one could disagree, least of all Huey Long.

Despite the verdict, Long claimed the judgment vindicated him of any serious wrongdoing. In addition, the trial had provided him with a unique and highly public forum from which to present his views. Indeed, his reputation as a reformer and maverick was only enhanced by the libel case against him. His standing across the state was elevated even further when he was elected chairman of the Public Service Commission later in the month.

One of his first actions as chairman involved reviewing a previous decision of the commission concerning a rate increase given to the Cumberland Telephone and Telegraph Company.

Long intended to reverse the ruling and force Cumberland to reduce the rate it charged its customers, the majority of whom lived in north Louisiana. The Cumberland case was complicated and time-consuming. At one point, Huey Long brought an aspect of the case all the way to the United States Supreme Court, which ruled in his favor.

Finally, on January 11, 1923, the case was settled when Huey and Cumberland reached a compromise. The commission would allow increases that averaged 50% of the company's original rate hike, a victory of sorts for Cumberland. However, the company was also required to return to its consumers a total of about $440,000, the difference between the old and new rates since the increase was put into effect, and to pay the commission about $20,000 to cover legal expenses and court costs. Huey Long had won the day.

"The victory is not one of self-interest but of public trust," stated one editorial in the New Orleans *Item*. "It is a victory of a public representative for the people." Indeed, every person who received a refund check from Cumberland—some 80,000 Louisiana voters—would remember the man who had made it possible: Huey P. Long.

On August 30, 1923, Huey Long turned 30. Finally, he was eligible to run for the office he felt born to hold: the governorship of Louisiana. He announced his candidacy that very day. The race between Louisiana's past and future had begun.

5

POLITICS AND RACE IN THE PELICAN STATE

> "Louisiana politics is of an intensity and complexity that are matched . . . only in the republic of Lebanon."
> — *A. J. Liebling*

In 1960, the journalist A. J. Liebling described the state of Louisiana during the gubernatorial campaign of Earl K. Long, Huey's younger brother. In doing so, he pointed to the striking division between north and south Louisiana by saying, "The balance between the Catholics in southern Louisiana and the Protestants in northern Louisiana is as delicate as that between the Moslems and Christians in Lebanon . . ." That division was only one of many unique elements of Louisiana's political and social make-up.

When Huey Long entered the governor's race in 1923, the political situation in Louisiana was even more complicated than Liebling described. In addition to the schism between north and south, there existed at least four other major divisions: between blacks and whites, rich and poor, Protestants and Catholics, and the urban and rural populations.

Perhaps the most deeply entrenched and ultimately destructive of these divisions was the one separating blacks from whites. Indeed, the seeds of social, political, and moral anguish were sown the moment the first white settler brought slaves onto the shores of the Mississippi River in the mid-1700s. From then on, the rich, fertile soil of Louisiana was contaminated by the insidious poison of racism. To fully understand Huey Long, his rise to power and, ultimately, his failure, it is important to examine the stormy and complicated history of race relations in Louisiana.

During its colonial history, control of what is today the state of Louisiana frequently passed between France and Spain as part of the enormous Louisiana Territory. The territory extended from the Mississippi River to the Rocky Mountains and from the Gulf of Mexico to British North America. Although Louisiana's greatest riches—oil, natural gas, and sulfur—lay deep beneath the earth and would not be uncovered for nearly two centuries, the colony had many other assets. First and foremost was the city of New Orleans, which sat upon the banks of the Mississippi River, North America's most important waterway. The colony also had an abundance of rich alluvial land suitable for growing cotton, sugar, and rice, three of the most valuable crops in the world.

Due to a scarcity of manpower and the labor-intensive quality of cotton and sugar cultivation, the slave trade expanded rapidly in Louisiana. Many blacks were brought to the colony directly from the African regions of Guinea, the Gold Coast, and Angola; others were taken from the French islands of the Caribbean. Altogether, about 32,000 black men and women were living in Louisiana when the territory was acquired from France by the United States in 1803; by the time the state of Louisiana, a small portion of the immense Louisiana Territory, officially became America's 18th state in 1812, the number of blacks had increased by several thousand.

Although most of the black immigrants were slaves, a substantial number were free blacks. In fact, Louisiana had the largest free black population in North America during the colonial period. Most free blacks worked as day laborers in New Orleans or existed as subsistence farmers or fishermen in the southern parishes. Most white Louisianians looked upon free people of color as a threat to slavery and severely restricted their rights. From early on, blacks—free or enslaved—were looked upon with suspicion and denigration by both poor and wealthy whites.

Until the United States Congress ordered a halt to the foreign slave trade in 1807, New Orleans was the most important slave market in the country. Following the ban, the smuggling of slaves continued on a fairly large scale for the remainder of the antebellum period. Among the most adept smugglers were the Baratarians, a group of people who lived on Grand Terre and Grand Isle at the mouth of Barataria Bay on the Gulf of Mexico. The leader of the Baratarians was the infamous pirate Jean LaFitte, who used the largely unmapped lacework of bayous to hide from the increasingly hostile United States military.

Until the Civil War, slavery cast an indelible shadow across Louisiana. White cotton and sugar plantation owners reaped the profits derived from the labor of slaves, the black men and women bought and sold as property to toil in the intense humidity of the lower Mississippi Valley. The breach between the races grew every day that this inhuman institution continued; racism, resentment, and fear became the predominant emotions between blacks and whites throughout Louisiana and much of the South.

Decades of increasing tension between Northern and Southern states over slavery finally reached a boiling point when Republican Abraham Lincoln was elected president of the United States in November 1860. Within six months, 11 Southern Democratic states, including Louisiana, formed the Confederate States of America and declared war on the Union. Louisiana's decision to secede and enter the war was far from unanimous, however. Many poor whites, especially in the northern part of the state, resented having to fight for an institution from which they derived nothing of any value. Nevertheless, Louisiana contributed its share of men and bullets to the bloody carnage of the Civil War.

The people of Louisiana were devastated—physically and spiritually—by the war and its aftermath. The state's banking system had been ruined, one half of its livestock had disappeared, and $170 million of its economic wealth (in the form of slaves) had been swept away by emancipation. Worst of all, the state had lost some 12,000 of its young men to bullets and disease.

Added to the economic misery were the social imperatives of the Confederate loss. Following the war, the world of the white Southerner was turned upside down. Blacks were set free and given the right to vote and hold public office. Most whites were disenfranchised, made to pay higher taxes, and forced to cede property to their Yankee vanquishers and their former slaves. Poor whites, who had few economic opportunities and only the social status that came by being white in a racist society, blamed the blacks for their sorry state of affairs.

To enforce the new social order, the Republican Party, the party of the victorious north, enacted the Military Reconstruction Act, which placed all former Confederate states under federal military control. Politics in the state became a contest between Yankee Republicans and Southern Democrats, a contest conducted with a fundamental disregard for moral or social ethics.

Stuffing ballot boxes, voting people dead and yet unborn, and making false returns had been fairly common practices throughout the state's history. During Reconstruction, however, such activities were elevated almost to an art form, with Democrats desperate to retain a measure of power and Republicans equally anxious to institute change and consolidate their newly claimed authority.

A crucial factor in the balance of power between Democrats and Republicans was black suffrage. The 15th Amendment, which granted the right to vote to all men, black and white, posed a special challenge to the Democrats. For the first time, blacks had the ability to fundamentally change their circumstances by voting candidates into office who would help them progress economically and politically. For the next several decades, the Democrats would use any and all methods, including violence and, eventually, legal disenfranchisement, to deny blacks this chance. First, however, they had to contend with the Northern Republicans who entered their state shortly after the end of the Civil War.

Louisiana's first Reconstruction governor was Henry Clay Warmoth, a former Union officer born and raised in Missouri. Tall, handsome, and exceedingly charming, Warmoth was singleminded in his determination to rule Louisiana. Ulysses S. Grant, under whom he served during the war, described him as "the shrewdest, boldest, ablest, and most conscienceless young man" he ever knew.

In order to move the Republican platform forward, Warmoth pressured the legislature to enact a series of laws that invested him with unprecedented authority. As governor, he was responsible for appointing nearly all local political offices, including parish constables, the militia, and the board of registration (which supervised all elections). Although Warmoth's measures were ostensibly meant to keep elections fair, many Democrats were certain that the Republicans were just as corrupt as they themselves were accused of being. As historian Joe Gray Taylor put it, "In all fairness . . . nobody can say with certainty who would have won if the elections had been honest, which none were."

Warmoth would have agreed with this assessment. "I don't pretend to be honest," Warmoth was quoted as saying soon after taking office, "I only pretend to be as honest as anybody in politics, and more so than those fellows who are opposing me now . . . Why, damn it, everybody is demoralized down here. Corruption is the fashion." Like Huey Long, who considered Warmoth a hero when he learned about him in school, Warmoth claimed he needed such far-reaching power in order to make the changes necessary in Louisiana society.

Indeed, the forces lining up against the Republicans and, specifically, the newly empowered blacks of the state were formidable.

Sometime during the spring and summer of 1868, a new and violent force emerged. The Knights of the White Camellia were modeled on the Ku Klux Klan, which had been organized in Tennessee the year before. Like the KKK, the Knights were a secret society of white supremacists. They wore masks to protect their identities and used intimidation and murder to prevent black voting. Their first campaign attempted to sway the November presidential election against Republican candidate General Ulysses S. Grant. They were quite successful; many parishes that had had substantial Republican majorities when the constitution was ratified in April polled few Republican votes in November. Although Grant won nationwide, Democrat Horatio Seymour carried Louisiana.

The Knights of the White Camellia and other less organized groups continued to terrorize blacks and any whites who showed support or sympathy for the blacks' cause. In Colfax, the seat of Grant Parish, a campaign to elect the parish sheriff turned into a bloody battle between whites and blacks; at least 63 black men were killed, including 25 prisoners in the local jail, who were executed on the spot.

Two years later, another white supremacist group formed. Called the White League, this organization operated as a paramilitary unit. Its members wore no masks, rode horses, and carried guns. Often the League had only to threaten blacks and white Republicans to obtain results. When intimidation failed, however, the White League did not shrink from carrying out their threats. In the town of Coushatta, they lynched five white Republicans who refused to resign their offices.

By September 1874, the White League controlled most of the rural parishes and towns. The state government, led by Republican William Pitt Kellogg, organized an integrated militia called the Metropolitan Police to protect itself and the city of New Orleans The situation came to a head in mid-September when a riot broke out at the foot of Canal Street in New Orleans; the White League members and the militia were armed with rifles and Gatling guns. Twenty-seven people were killed and more than 100 wounded. The Battle of Liberty Place was long remembered by the whites of Louisiana as a great victory, the time when "citizens fell fighting for free government."

Although Governor Kellogg remained in office, protected by federal troops, for another two years, the Battle of Liberty Place marked the end of Reconstruction efforts in Louisiana. In 1877, the official end of Reconstruction occurred when President Rutherford B. Hayes withdrew federal troops from the three states still under federal control: Louisiana, Florida, and South Carolina. Without military support and protection, the Republican Party crumbled. The Democrats, or Bourbons, as they were now called, took control throughout much of the South.

In Louisiana, this conservative coalition was made up of cotton and sugar planters in the countryside and wealthy bankers, brokers, and merchants in New Orleans. The Louisiana Bourbon Democrats held fast to three main principles: First, government should play a very small role in the lives of Louisiana citizens; thus, funding for schools, roads, and other public facilities should be drastically limited. To that end, a new constitution was created in 1879. This document significantly reduced property taxes, made it difficult for the state to borrow money to fund public works, and slashed the budget for education.

The second main point in the Democratic creed was white supremacy. Although Reconstruction never completely upset the social order of the South, it did legally entitle blacks to participate in the political process. By federal law, blacks had the right to vote and the Bourbons were not about to risk federal intervention in their affairs by denying them outright. Instead, they continued to use the method that had worked for them during Reconstruction: fear and intimidation. In fact, the New Orleans branch of the White League, the terrorist organization that fought the Battle of Liberty Place, served as the legal militia of the state during the late 1880s and 1890s.

The Bourbons made good use of the black votes they kept from being cast by simply counting them as votes for the Democrats. This practice resulted in topsy-turvy election results: The parishes with the largest numbers of blacks turned in the highest vote tallies for the Democrats, the party of white supremacy. "A dead darky always makes a good Democrat," went a common expression, "and never ceases to vote."

A third tenet of Bourbon rule held that poor blacks and poor whites must be kept from recognizing and acting upon their common interests; if they were ever to join forces, they would certainly outnumber and thus defeat the ruling elite. In order to retain power, then, the Bourbon Democrats often resorted to actively encouraging racial animosity. To vote for anyone other than a traditional Democrat, claimed the Bourbons, was to risk a return to those days when the poor white farmer held an even lower position on the social and economic ladder than he did under the Democrats.

For the next decade or so, the Bourbon Democrats maintained almost complete control of Louisiana government. In New Orleans, the Bourbons formed a unique alliance with a company first brought to Louisiana during Reconstruction. Chartered as a monopoly in 1868, the Louisiana State Lottery was a private gambling venture that forged a relationship with the wealthy merchants and politicians of the city. When it became clear that the Bourbons would soon come to power, the Lottery contributed heavily to whichever candidate it felt would best protect its interests. The Lottery also dispensed bribes to state politicians and newspaper editors and reporters. When the Lottery joined with a group of politicians in New Orleans called the Ring, a powerful political machine was born that would affect Louisiana politics until well into the 20th century. Corruption became the rule rather than the exception in Louisiana government.

Under the Bourbons, the state economy languished, public services were nearly nonexistent, and the majority of Louisianians, both black and white, sunk deeper into poverty. Modern industry came more slowly to Louisiana than it did to the rest of the country; thus more of its people were struggling to exist as subsistence farmers and sharecroppers. Moreover, government funding of education, health care, road construction, and other public services had fallen to below pre-Civil War levels in many areas of the state.

Out of these conditions, the first challenge to Bourbon rule arose in the late 1880s and early 1890s when the Populist movement began to gain momentum among farmers in the mid-West and South. In addition to challenging the economic policies of the Bourbon Democrats, the Populists also threatened the racial status quo. The Populist platform shocked Bourbon sensibilities: "We declare emphatically that the interests of the white and colored races in the South are identical . . . equal justice and fairness must be accorded to each."

As well as attracting the poor white and black farmers, the Louisiana Populist Party drew support among a traditional source of Democratic power: the wealthy sugar planters of the southern part of the state. Sugar planters were upset with the state and national Democratic Party because of President Grover Cleveland's refusal to support tariff protection for sugar growers.

Although the Populist movement failed in both its national and statewide efforts during the 1890s, the ruling elite in Louisiana felt threatened by its widespread popularity. No longer as fearful of federal intervention, as they had been immediately following Reconstruction, the Bourbons acted quickly and decisively to ensure that another coalition did not threaten their power in the future.

In 1890, the state enacted its first segregation law. It required that all railroads carrying passengers in Louisiana provide "separate but equal" accommodations for whites and blacks. Although the law was contested by angry blacks in Louisiana, the United States Supreme Court declared the law constitutional in the landmark case, *Plessy v. Ferguson*. Violence against blacks continued unabated; Louisiana ranked fourth in the number of lynchings that occurred every year, behind Mississippi, Georgia, and Texas. After the *Plessy* decision, segregation became a legal and widespread way of life in Louisiana and throughout the South.

In 1898, the Bourbon Democrats consolidated their power further by creating a new constitution. In essence, the constitution of 1898 disenfranchised all blacks—thereby effectively cancelling the 15th Amendment in Louisiana—and, to a lesser degree, poor whites. In order to vote, one had to demonstrate the ability to read and write in his native language—a rare occurrence in a state in which more than 40% of its whites and even more of its blacks were illiterate during this period—or show a property assessment of not less than $300. Poor and/or illiterate whites had one additional chance to earn suffrage: If they could prove that their father or grandfather had voted in Louisiana before 1867—before military Reconstruction—they would be allowed to vote. This was called the grandfather clause. A poll tax of $1 per year was also levied and a voter had to show receipts for two years' payment when he appeared at the precinct.

Such measures resulted in dramatically reduced voting rolls throughout the state. The number of white voters dropped from about 164,000 in 1897 to 92,000 in 1904; black registration fell from 130,344 to 1,342 in the same period. In 1922, only 598 black voters were listed in Louisiana, while the number of white voters had increased to about 145,000. This increase was largely due to the addition of women to the voting rolls after the 19th Amendment to the U.S. Constitution was passed in 1920.

During this period, a force that had lain somewhat dormant since Reconstruction reemerged in many Southern states, including Louisiana. The Ku Klux Klan, a secret society committed to the maintenance of white supremacy, reorganized in 1915 and rapidly extended both its membership and its targets: By the early 1920s, the KKK claimed nearly five million members nationwide and added Catholics, Jews, pacifists, foreigners, and any white people who dared to live "irregular lives" to its list of enemies. Wearing hoods and masks, members of the KKK set fire to stores and homes, burned crosses on lawns, and, often, resorted to murder in order to terrorize those they considered "unworthy of calling themselves Americans."

Louisiana had relatively few Klan members—about 25,000 at the height of Klan influence—largely due to the high percentage of Catholics who lived in the state. In the northwestern, largely Protestant parishes, however, a KKK stronghold began to develop in the early 1920s. Centered in Shreveport, an overwhelmingly Protestant and conservative city, the Louisiana Klan attracted business and political leaders. The pastor of the city's largest church also endorsed the organization, claiming that it stood for "nationality, race and religion . . . the deepest, highest, and mightiest motives of man." In 1922, a Klan member became Shreveport's mayor.

The presence of the Ku Klux Klan further divided Louisiana. The Catholic parishes of the south reacted with outrage when Klan violence in the north occurred. When anti-Klan men were murdered in Morehouse Parish, Governor Parker went so far as to ask the federal government for help in controlling the Klan in late 1922. "These conditions are beyond the control of the Governor of this State," he wrote to the president. Members of the newly formed Federal Bureau of Investigation arrived to investigate and Parker sent national guardsmen to restore peace.

Such was the situation in Louisiana when the gubernatorial race of 1924 began. An entrenched ruling class, the Bourbon Democrats, with a long history of manipulating the votes of poor whites as well as blacks, controlled much of the state. In addition, racial and religious discord had reached an all-time high, pitting blacks against whites and northern Protestants against southern Catholics. Attempting to break the power of the Bourbons and heal the rifts between blacks and whites and Protestants and Catholics was a 30-year-old man from Winn Parish named Huey P. Long.

6

THE RACE FOR GOVERNOR
Campaigning for the Gubernatorial Office:
1923–1928

> "I was born into politics a wedded man,
> with a storm for my bride."
> —*Huey P. Long*

This state shows every need for a constructive administration, devoted to the protection and expansion of labor and
capital, industry and agriculture, all working toward the
efficiency of our courts, public schools, freedom in religious
beliefs, and reduction in taxation and burdens of government, and toward liberating our state and our institutions
from the ever growing modern tendency of monopoly and
concentration of power.

So read Huey Long's statement to the press announcing
his candidacy for the office of governor. In it, he raised
issues of genuine importance to the people of Louisiana,
particularly the need for economic expansion and better
schools. During his campaign, Long would expand on these
themes, raise others, and spread his message to every part of
the state with characteristic energy and charisma.

Long's ability to sway the voters of the state was hampered
by the two main challenges to his candidacy: the control of the
political scene by traditional Democrats and the explosive issue
of the Ku Klux Klan. He attempted to devise strategies to meet
them both.

As far as the Bourbons were concerned, Long decided to
attack their grip on power on a local level, parish by parish.
Every parish had its own political leader, usually the sheriff or

other local official, who was in charge of garnering the vote of the parish population for one of the Democratic candidates. The candidate who controlled the most number of parish leaders, therefore, usually won the election. "I'll tell you how I'm going to win," Huey told a newspaper reporter early in 1923:

> In every parish there is a boss, usually the sheriff. He has 40 percent of the votes, 40 percent are opposed to him, and 20 percent are in between. I'm going into every parish and cuss out the boss. That gives me 40 percent of the vote to begin with and I will horse trade the boss out of the in-betweens.

Long also planned to employ this tactic on a larger scale by attacking "bosses" on a statewide and national level. Anyone who held power, from present Louisiana Governor John Parker to John D. Rockefeller of the Standard Oil Company, was the enemy of the ordinary citizens of Louisiana, he believed.

Long's strategy would hit a major obstacle in New Orleans, the state's largest city. The Democrats held the reins of power in New Orleans through a highly efficient organization known as the Old Regulars, which had developed out of the Lottery-Ring element active in the 1870s and 1880s. A coalition of big-city politicians, businessmen, and rural cotton planters, the Old Regulars represented the single most powerful voice in state politics during this period.

Led by Martin Behrman, who also served as mayor of New Orleans from 1904 until 1920, the Old Regulars determined what candidates the city would nominate and what stand the parish of Orleans would take on issues in the state legislature. It did so by any means necessary, including padding voting rolls with false names and paying the poll taxes of large numbers of poor people and voting them in blocks.

A primary goal of the Old Regulars was to maintain control of the city and its resources. It opposed state regulation of utilities and lowered taxes on business property. Under the Regulars, New Orleans' long-entrenched vice thrived; Mayor Behrman, a heavy-set man with a burly, toothbrush moustache, was reported to have said, "You can make prostitution illegal in Louisiana, but you can't make it unpopular."

The alliance between urban and rural interests represented by the Old Regulars was a new one in Louisiana; early in the state's history, rural and urban interests were diametrically opposed to one another. Since disenfranchisement, when blacks were denied the right to vote through state legislation, however, the Democrats in the countryside were unable to count on obtaining many fraudulent votes from rural blacks. They now depended on a friendly New Orleans machine that would support their conservative interests and deliver a majority of the city's vote. The ruthlessness with which the Old Regulars pursued their goals made it difficult for a rival or reform faction within or outside the Democratic party to come to power.

As he approached his first gubernatorial race, Huey Long realized he would have difficulty gaining support in New Orleans. He could not count on 40% of New Orleans citizens voting against "the boss," which in this case was the Old Regulars, or even having their votes properly counted if they did decide to support him. Indeed, throughout his political career, the Crescent City, as New Orleans was known, would remain nearly impenetrable to Long's own machinations.

As for coping with his state's deep racial and ethnic divisions, Huey Long planned to do what few men before him had attempted: By focusing on broader themes, and ignoring religious and racial issues, Huey intended to unite the majority of voters in both north and south Louisiana. He would appeal to the hard-scrabble Baptist farmers in the north, the poor French fisherman in the bayous, and the beleaguered employees of big lumber and oil companies across the state. As for the blacks, Huey Long would attempt to leave them out of the equation altogether, mainly because they could not vote. By bringing black issues into the campaign, Huey would only risk alienating white voters in the state.

One handbill for the campaign summed up the spirit Huey Long hoped to engender in the people of his state who could vote: "We are for Huey P. Long because he is the poor man's friend and has the manhood and courage to defend the rights of the people." Many voters in the state remembered Huey Long as a maverick who had fought and won against Standard Oil, Cumberland Telephone and Telegraph, and other big-business interests.

Long's opponents in this race, on the other hand, were more traditional politicians. Henry L. Fuqua, a Protestant from south Louisiana, was then serving as director of the state penitentiary at Angola. Although he was not a particularly inspiring speaker, the heavy-set man with a pudgy face had the backing of the Old Regulars and many south Louisiana parish leaders. With his Protestant background, he could expect to draw significant support in north Louisiana as well.

The third candidate in the 1923 gubernatorial race was Hewitt Bouanchard, a Catholic Frenchman from Pointe Coupee Parish in south Louisiana. Bouanchard had the support of the current governor, John Parker, as well as the "New Regulars," a group of businessmen and politicians organized to oppose the Old Regulars in New Orleans. Described as a "cold drink of water" by the New Regulars' chairman, John P. Sullivan, Bouanchard lacked the charisma so important to successful politicians.

Huey Long faced formidable opposition in these two candidates, both of whom had strong, organized political support. Had blacks been able to vote, Long might have followed in the footsteps of traditional Populists and attempted to unite the poor people of both races. By doing so, he might have succeeded in attracting an overwhelming—and unbeatable—majority of the state's citizens. As things stood, however, Long's own appeal was limited to poor white people, many of whom could not afford to vote for him because of the poll tax, and a few country parish leaders in the north.

In New Orleans, Long received some help from yet another new group opposing the Old Regulars. Called the Independent Regulars, this organization was formed by Francis Williams, a colleague of Huey's on the Public Service Commission. With few members and little power in the city, the Independent Regulars could not be counted on to bring in many votes for its candidate. Huey, however, believed he could win without a powerful New Orleans machine behind him; he told Williams, "Give me a handful of city votes—no more than 15,000, and I'm as good as elected."

It is impossible to predict how Huey Long might have fared had 1923 been a less volatile year in Louisiana politics. Unfortunately, the Klan issue overshadowed all other aspects of the campaign. Huey and his opponents faced the same dilemma:

To come out strongly against the Klan would be to alienate the Protestants in the north; to support the organization would mean losing the votes of the southern parishes, where a majority of Catholics lived. In either case, victory would be unlikely.

Each candidate took a slightly different tack. Fuqua supported enacting laws that would ban the public wearing of hoods and masks by organization members—without masks, members risked being identified by the people they harassed—but avoided strongly denouncing the group. Many people believed that he had the support of high-ranking, wealthy members of the organization in the north. Bouanchard, on the other hand, was an outspoken enemy of the Klan. Claiming he would "put it out of business," he was assured of consolidating his support among the Catholics in the south.

Simply by being a Protestant from the north, Huey Long was suspected of having strong Klan sympathies, if not of actually being a Klan member himself. He had recognized this danger some time before, writing to his brother George in 1921: "I am not a member [of the Klan], and while I have never taken a line either way, I requested some of my good friends whom I know to be members that I not be asked to join." Since George himself was active in the Klan in Oklahoma, Huey's statements to him are especially revealing.

Without doubt, Huey Long was racist; he thought that whites were superior to blacks and that blacks deserved the low position they held in society. He frequently referred to blacks as "niggers" and never went out of his way politically to help them in their struggle for civil and human rights. On the other hand, he did not appear to hate blacks with the vehemence of many of his Southern compatriots, nor did he propose measures to further debase or abuse them. On this, as on most other issues, Long was an opportunist; his brother Julius said that Huey would "claim to have negro blood in him" if he thought it would get him any negro votes.

As for Catholics, the other target of Klan wrath, Long did not seem to harbor any particular religious enmity. He was, however, generally unaccustomed to the southern Louisiana way of life; like many of his northern neighbors, he mistrusted the easy-going manners, bon vivant lifestyle, and generally more tolerant racial attitudes of the southerners. He would have to work hard to accept and be accepted in the southern parishes.

Long's attempt to straddle the Klan issue in 1923 confused voters in both regions of the country. At one point in the campaign, he told the Shreveport *Times*, "In north Louisiana they have me in league with the holy people of Rome, in south Louisiana they picture me in a hood and nightgown." Instead of further explaining his point of view, he tried to focus the discussion on other issues. To Huey, it was a waste of time "to have one poor man fighting another poor man while the corporations are starving the children of both."

Although he often used his most effective technique—insulting his opponents and supporters—Long spent much time describing the positive things he would do if and when he became governor. One of his major concerns was the sorry state of Louisiana's educational system. In 1920, Louisiana had the highest illiteracy rate in the country, with more than 20% of its people unable to read or write. Its schools, especially those in poor, rural areas, were sparsely staffed and without basic supplies. Schoolbooks were sold, at often exorbitant costs that few families could afford; moreover, they were revised nearly

Huey Long promised to "take Louisiana out of the mud" by building new roads throughout the state. Here, a road is being constructed through a northern Louisiana parish in 1937. (Louisiana State Library)

every year, making "hand-me-downs" among family members impractical. When he became governor, Huey proposed, he would provide free textbooks to all children, black and white, who attended public school as well as those enrolled in private Catholic schools. He would also demand that the legislature increase state support for public schools.

Long also promised to significantly increase spending on highway and bridge construction. The need for improved roads throughout the state had been evident even before the first automobile appeared in Louisiana in 1899. As automobiles became more affordable and the population a bit more prosperous after World War I, voters by the thousands began to complain of poor road conditions. Long insisted that the state had failed in its responsibility to provide safe and durable roadways saying, "We continue to wade in the mud where we had expected asphalt."

Huey Long made another promise to his potential supporters: He would not only improve schools, build roads and bridges, and expand the government's role in providing public services of all kinds, but he would do all this without raising taxes. By eliminating fraud and extravagance, the government would be run more efficiently and economically. The money saved would then be spent on projects that would mean the most to the poor and working people of Louisiana.

Although Long's proposals may sound familiar and mainstream today, they were considered radical and threatening to the traditional Democrats of 1923. He was frequently called a Bolshevik or communist for advocating increased state responsibility for the welfare of its citizens; Lenin and other members of the Bolshevik Party had established the first communist government in the new Soviet Union a few years earlier after a bloody revolution. Despite the fact that conditions in the United States were fundamentally different from those that provoked the Soviet uprising—this country was both politically and economically far more stable—it was easy to raise fears of a similar turn of events in the United States.

In addition to mistrusting his politics, many traditional politicians were appalled by Huey's country-style manners and vulgar language. (Ironically, it was his ability to "speak American," as journalist Hamilton Basso noted, that most attracted the majority of voters.) Most important of all, Huey Long was

Huey Long brought his message to the smallest, most isolated villages and towns in his state. Here, he delivers a speech at a typical campaign stop. (Louisiana State Library)

one of the first Louisiana politicians of the 20th century who could not be controlled by the Old Regulars or any other machine or individual. The powers-that-be in state government recognized Huey for what he was: a loose cannon.

As he did during his campaign for Railroad Commissioner, Long traveled extensively into the smallest towns in Louisiana, reaching as many of his potential constituents as possible. In New Orleans, he became the first candidate in Louisiana history to use the radio as a way to get his message across by broadcasting a speech; the technology to do so had only been available for three years. Unfortunately, just 8,000 people owned radios in the city at the time.

Huey's face appeared on thousands of leaflets and circulars along with his campaign slogan: LONG OUR NEXT GOVERNOR; they were posted all over the state. One of his favorite locations was the inside window of a barbershop. He figured that the men waiting to be served would have little to do but stare at his name and his face; when election day came, they would certainly remember Huey P. Long.

Huey's energy seemed boundless. He made five speeches a day or more, each one passionate and exuberant. He flailed his arms, paced across the platform, and often removed his tie and loosened his shirt. As one witness said to a Long supporter at a rally, "I like your friend, but I was worried. I didn't know what he was going to take off next." When he spoke about issues especially close to him, such as the "invisible empire of Standard Oil," his usually clear and resonant voice became high and raspy. By the end of a particularly busy day, he would lose his voice altogether.

Slowly but steadily, Huey Long began to increase support for his candidacy and his programs among voters across the state. He had more difficulty with members of the press, particularly the reporters and editors of the New Orleans newspapers, the *States,* the *Item,* and the *Times-Picayune.* One *Times-Picayune* editorial referred to Huey as a "singularly uninformed buffoon." The *Item*'s cartoonist portrayed him in a court jester costume and labeled him "the Prince of Piffle."

Long used the negative press to expand on one of his most familiar themes: corporate control of the state. Newspapers, claimed Huey, were told what to print by their corporate owners and most of what they printed were lies. "There is as much honor in the New Orleans *Item* as there is in the heel of a flea," Huey declaimed on September 19, 1923. The relationship between Huey Long and the press would never be a friendly one, but the breach between them in Long's first statewide election was particularly damaging; without the press behind him, Long had little chance of building support among more traditional Louisiana citizens.

Election day, January 15, 1924, was cold and rainy. Despite the weather, nearly 240,000 Louisianans voted. When the returns were counted, conservative Louisiana found they had reason to worry about the young upstart from Winn Parish: Although Huey Long ran third, he earned just about 10,000 votes fewer than the leading candidate, Henry Fuqua. Bouanchard came in second, about 1,000 votes behind Fuqua; Bouanchard would eventually lose to Fuqua in the February runoff.

What alarmed the ruling elite most about Long's showing was the distribution of his votes; Huey won in all but six of the parishes in the north-central and southeastern part of the state. He polled a majority of votes in 21 parishes and a plurality in seven. And most of his supporters had one thing in common: they were small farmers or workers and poor. As T. Harry Williams, professor of history at Louisiana State University from 1941 until his death in 1979, wrote in his landmark biography of Huey Long, "For the first time the masses of Louisiana had rallied behind a leader, and it was terrifyingly evident that they realized their power and that they liked the sensation."

Never able to admit defeat gracefully, Huey Long claimed, "I have only the rains to blame for not being the next governor." Despite his glib remark, Huey learned a great deal from his first attempt to win the governorship. He now saw his weaknesses clearly; the next time he ran, he would have to either break the New Orleans machine (he scored a paltry 12,000 votes in the city) or score better among the southern parishes. "We have only begun to fight," he told the New Orleans *Item*.

Long's next campaign began practically as soon as the returns from his first were counted. First on his agenda was winning reelection to the Public Service Commission, which he accomplished handily in September 1924 by winning nearly 84% of the total vote. His second term on the commission would be far less volatile than his first, however, for three main reasons.

First, the major corporations under the commission's domain were now well aware of their responsibilities and thus required less prodding by Huey and his colleagues. Second, Huey had his eyes on a bigger prize—the governor's chair—and he let nothing stand between him and a successful race in 1928. Third, within two years, the balance of power on the three-man commission would tilt away from Huey. Once he was removed from his chairmanship, he rarely attended commission meetings at all.

Instead, Long concentrated on increasing his visibility and appeal in southern Louisiana and, to a lesser degree, New Orleans. To do so, he involved himself in two statewide Senate campaigns, the first in the spring of 1924 and the second in 1926. Both candidates, Joseph Ransdell and Edwin Broussard, were Catholic and from the southern part of the state. By campaigning for them, Huey endeared himself to their many

Catholic and French supporters. At the same, he used every available opportunity to let the southerners know he would be running for governor again. One French fisherman recounts his first experience with Huey Long the campaigner and candidate in broken English derived from the French patois known as Cajun:

> Right away he start to tell about Huey Long, yeh, what fine man he is, what fine governor he make some day. And I wonder, me, why he no say something about Broussard . . . I just bout get mad, yeh, an go for to leave, when he say Edwin Broussard is fine man, ablest man in the Senate.

On August 3, 1927, Huey Long officially announced his candidacy at a rally in Shreveport. Huey's campaign slogan, "Everyman a King But No One Wears a Crown," was printed on an enormous banner behind the dais in the auditorium. Paraphrased from a speech by William Jennings Bryan, Democratic leader and orator, in 1896, the slogan attempted to express Huey's fundamental philosophy: that the poor of the state had a right to a better life, a life that had been denied them by the rich individuals and corporations who, until now, controlled the government. With Huey Long in the governor's chair, there would be free schoolbooks for every child in the state, highways and bridges throughout every parish, and less corruption in the halls of the legislature.

Although his message was almost identical to the one he had espoused four years before, the political scene in Louisiana was radically different. The powerful head of the Old Regulars, Martin Behrman, had died the year before, leaving the organization in a temporarily weakened position. The Ku Klux Klan had all but disappeared, as both an issue and an organization, since Governor Fuqua had enacted an antimasking law in 1925. Governor Fuqua himself had passed away, leaving his far less popular lieutenant governor, Oramel Simpson, in charge.

In the years between campaigns, Huey had also been able to solidify significant financial and political support. In addition to his family, Long received substantial contributions from several New Orleans and Shreveport businessmen. Robert S.

Maestri, one of the wealthiest men in New Orleans, was the largest contributor to the Long campaign, donating or loaning Long hundreds of thousands of dollars. All contributions to Huey's campaign chest were made in cash, as was every expenditure made by him or his supporters. Later, his unconventional bookkeeping would cause him no end of trouble.

Huey also had the support of both Louisiana senators, Broussard and Ransdell, for whom he had campaigned. Even the parish leaders he had so vehemently attacked in the last campaign were beginning to support Huey Long, probably because most of the people in their parishes supported him. "They fell in line," said one official. "The people were for him." Hoping to make some headway into New Orleans, Huey also forged an alliance with the New Regulars, whose most important journalistic voice was Long's former nemesis, the New Orleans *States*.

In addition, Huey faced far less formidable candidates than he had in the last campaign. Oramel Simpson, the sitting governor, borrowed much of Long's own platform for his campaign, promising free schoolbooks and a more extensive highway construction program. Simpson, however, was a poor public speaker and reputedly addicted to alcohol; even the Old Regulars who had elected Fuqua decided not to support Simpson.

Long's other opponent was Riley J. Wilson, Louisiana's Eighth District congressman and a staunch conservative in the Bourbon tradition. Known as Riley Joe to his constituents, Wilson had successfully lobbied for federal intervention during the state's worst natural disaster in history, a flood that had covered one-third of the state the previous spring. Huey made good use of this information to attack his opponent. Wilson, he claimed, "has been in Congress for fourteen years and this year the water went fourteen feet higher than ever before, giving him a flood record of one foot of high water to the year, if that's what he's claiming credit for." Flood control itself was an important issue in the campaign, with all of the candidates supporting increased federal funds to pay for levees, spillways, and other methods to control the Mississippi.

One of the most impressive and moving speeches Huey Long made during this campaign occurred in the little town of St. Martinsville, Evangeline Parish, south Louisiana. There, he brought to life the spirit of the first Acadian settlers, whose journey to Louisiana was commemorated by a Henry Wadsworth Longfellow poem:

> And it is here under this oak where Evangeline waited for her lover, Gabriel who never came. This oak is an immortal spot, made so by Longfellow's poem, but Evangeline is not the only one who has waited here in disappointment. Where are the schools that you have waited for your children to have, that have never come? Where are the roads and the highways that you send your money to build, that are no nearer now than ever before? Where are the institutions to care for the sick and disabled? Evangeline wept bitter tears in her disappointment, but it lasted only one lifetime. Your tears in this country, around this oak, have lasted for generations. Give me the chance to dry the eyes of those who still weep here.

The people of Louisiana gave Huey Long that chance. On election day, January 17, 1928, the sun shone and the weather was warm. Long garnered 126,842 votes, Wilson earned 81,747, and Simpson came in third, with 80,236. Huey carried six of the eight congressional districts and 47 of the 64 parishes. Although he lacked a majority of the popular vote, he had a bigger lead than any past gubernatorial candidate. Wilson, who soon realized he had no chance of beating Huey in the runoff, withdrew his name. In April, the runoff election, in which fewer voters participated, went as expected in a Democratic state like Louisiana: Long won 92,941 votes to his Republican opponent's paltry 3,733.

Huey Long had achieved what seemed almost unthinkable to the conservatives even four years before: He became governor of Louisiana. At just under 35 years of age, Huey was the youngest governor in the history of the state and he was far from finished. "Stick by me," Huey told his campaign staff, "We'll show 'em who's boss. I'm going to be president someday."

7

FIGHTING FIRE WITH FIRE
Long as Governor and the Impeachment Fight: 1928–1929

"There may be smarter men than me, but they ain't in Louisiana."

—*Huey P. Long*

A crowd 15,000 strong witnessed Huey Long's inauguration in Baton Rouge on May 21, 1928. Men, women, and children from all over the state gathered on the sunny, muggy day to watch a morning parade featuring the new governor, who, with "half his body . . . through the window of the car . . . waved both his arms" at the enthusiastic crowd of well-wishers. "How he was prevented from falling out of the car," noted one witness, "is beyond me."

In the afternoon, concerts and barbecues were held throughout the city; in the evening, a reception and inaugural ball toasted the new governor. In a true spirit of democracy, no tickets were required for any of the festivities: Rich and poor alike were welcome throughout the state capital that day. Huey Long, who once said that he would "rather be the biggest man in a little village than the second biggest man in a great city," now was the biggest man in his home state of Louisiana.

With him in the car were his wife and three children: Rose, who was the eldest at 11; Russell, aged 10; and three-year-old Palmer Reed, who was born the day Huey was indicted for libel in 1924. In fact, Palmer Reed was named for the two attorneys who defended their client with relative success. His children, who had "learned almost by the time they could walk to fold and mail literature for campaigns," as Huey wrote in his autobiography, must have been almost excited as their father at the attention given to the first family that day.

By this time, the Longs had moved into the governor's mansion, a rambling, antebellum-style house in the capital city. From the start, Huey Long hated his new home, perhaps because its traditional style reminded him of the powerful forces of the past that still gripped the state. He reportedly told a colleague that he found it "galling to live in a house that John Parker and Ruffin Pleasant had occupied." It was also drafty, leaky, and infested with termites. Within several days, Rose and the children had returned to their home in Shreveport and Huey had taken up almost permanent residence in the Heidelberg Hotel, located close to the capitol building.

Dislike of the governor's mansion was only one reason for Rose Long to depart for Shreveport, where she and the children would remain most of the time. What disturbed Rose most was trying to live with a husband who once told her quite frankly, "I can't live a normal family life." Huey's irregular habits would have been trying enough, including as they did bouts of insomnia and a penchant for carousing in New Orleans nightclubs. In addition, however, Huey also had a mistress, a young woman named Alice Lee Grosjean.

Twenty-two-years old in 1928, Grosjean had been hired as Huey's personal secretary during his first gubernatorial campaign in 1924. A pretty, petite woman who did not divorce her husband, James Terrell, until late 1928, Alice soon became one of Huey's closest confidantes. That the two had a romantic affair is undocumented, but not in much doubt. In fact, Huey had the audacity to offer living quarters in the governor's mansion to Alice when they first arrived in the capital, an act that certainly affected Rose's decision to leave for Shreveport. When Huey moved to the Heidelberg Hotel, Alice accompanied him, taking a suite just a few doors down the hall from her employer.

Rose Long never spoke of Alice in public, but relations between the Longs remained strained throughout Huey's life; Rose and the children were seen with the governor only on rare occasions. By this time, Huey and other members of his family suffered under similar tension. "I'd like to get as far away from my damn kinfolks as I could," Huey bluntly told a friend. He rarely saw his father nor, according to his brothers, did he contribute to Old Hu's support. Huey only sporadically helped provide for his sister Callie, who was ill with asthma and lived in Arizona, or visited with his other sisters.

As for his brothers, Huey remained suspicious of all three. Relations between Julius and the governor were particularly strained and would grow increasingly bitter with time. Huey's break with George over the Klan issue was never breached and the brothers rarely saw each other. Only Earl, the youngest of the Longs, had a close personal and political relationship with Huey.

"That little brother of mine is the hottest-headed, meanest man," Huey said of Earl, "but to be frank, I owe a lot of my success to him." Two years younger, but always heavier and stronger than Huey, Earl had long served as his brother's protector and promoter. When the two were children, Earl often finished fist fights that Huey had instigated but had no desire to partake in; "I don't think Huey liked to fight," Earl, who appeared to rather enjoy using his fists, later remembered.

As adults, Huey and Earl, who was also a lawyer, formed a unique and largely successful relationship. Although Huey claimed never to fully trust his younger brother, he awarded Earl choice jobs in his administration and counted on his efforts to rally support for his programs among both legislators and constituents.

"Huey was a more refined politician," a former mayor of the city of Breaux Bridge observed. "Earl dressed and acted like one of us Cajuns. But he had more friends." Later, Earl would use his remarkable abilities to forge his own memorable political career. For now, he joined his brother in the capital as Huey prepared to assume control of the government.

Huey's rambunctious personality and radical politics had earned him very few political friends in Baton Rouge. Fortunately, two trustworthy allies would be joining him in the capital: Oscar K. Allen and Harley Bozeman, both childhood friends from Winnfield, had won election to the state Senate and House of Representatives, respectively. In addition to having genuine affection for the new governor, Allen and Bozeman pledged their loyalty to Long in exchange for prominent government posts that they would hold concurrently with their elective offices.

Four other men joined Huey Long's inner circle in 1928. Seymour Weiss, owner of the Roosevelt Hotel in New Orleans, became one of Long's closest associates. As well as providing Huey with an elegant suite in the hotel, Weiss had served as unofficial treasurer of the Long organization during the gubernatorial race, a position he would maintain while Huey was in office. John Sullivan, who headed the New Regulars in New Orleans, Colonel Robert Ewing, the owner of the only two New Orleans' newspapers that supported Huey Long, and Robert Maestri, the wealthy businessman who had donated funds to the campaign, were also given wide access to the new governor in return for their past and, hopefully, future support.

Huey and his advisers faced formidable opposition: Only 18 out of 100 members of the House of Representatives and nine out of 39 senators had supported Huey Long for governor. If Huey wanted to see his programs enacted, he would have to win the votes, if not the hearts, of politicians who had so far opposed him. To do so, he used methods many considered ruthless.

"I'm fighting a crooked machine in the Old Regulars," Huey said in defense of his actions, "and I have to fight fire with fire. I'm going to build a better machine." He started construction on his new machine immediately after the election. After making a list of legislators who might be open to persuasion, he asked Bozeman and Allen to convince these men to pledge their support to the new governor and to vote the "Long way" in the legislature. By Huey's inauguration in May, Bozeman and Allen were able to report that Long now had a majority of lawmakers on his side in both houses.

Exactly how they were able to bring the legislators over to the Long camp was never documented, but without doubt certain promises were made. "They all didn't come free," as Bozeman later admitted. Some were offered positions of power in the legislature; others were probably bought with hard cash. Most, however, were promised jobs for themselves, their relatives, or the people who lived in the parishes they represented, in agencies and boards that administered the state business, a practice known as patronage.

Every governor of Louisiana since the state was admitted to the Union had used patronage to one degree or another. Huey Long, however, raised the practice to an art form. First, he appointed Long supporters to head every agency legally under the governor's domain; Huey appointed state Senator O. K. Allen, for instance, chairman of the powerful Highway Commission and thus, through Allen, controlled the hundreds of jobs the commission supervised.

When rules denied him the right to make appointments, Huey did what he had always done in the past: He changed the rules to get what he wanted. A typical example of his resolve involved the Levee Board of Orleans Parish, which oversaw the upkeep of the dikes that protected New Orleans from being flooded by the Mississippi River. With one of the largest employment rolls in the state, the Levee Board was made up of nine members appointed for fixed terms. These men could not be removed before their terms were up, even by the new governor.

Instead of obeying the law, Huey decided to simply change it; he pressured the legislature into enacting a bill that dissolved the old board and created a new five-member body. Four of the five new members were loyal Long men, the fifth was the former president of the board Huey allowed to stay on as a small concession to the opposition. Using similarly cutthroat methods, Huey gained control over the jobs and services supervised by the Board of Health, the Conservation Commission, the Charity Hospital of New Orleans, and many others.

Using the promise of some 25,000 lucrative state jobs along with the power of his own personality, Long managed to fundamentally change the face of government in a very short time. At the opening session of the legislature in May 1928, Long men were elected to be the presiding officers of the Senate and House: Philip Gilbert became president *pro tem* of the Senate and John Fournet won the election for speaker of the House. Through these two men, Huey continued to build his machine.

According to the rules of the legislature, the president of the Senate and the speaker of the House could choose who in each house would sit on the law-making committees. Under Huey's direction, Gilbert and Fournet stacked the committees with legislators they believed were loyal to Long; Harley Bozeman, for instance, was made chairman of the important House appropriations committee.

Huey went one step further. To ensure the continued support of the men he placed in positions of power, Huey required them to write—and sign—their own resignations. The threat behind such an act was implicit: At the first sign of dissent, Huey could simply fill in the date to make a resignation official. The dissident government employee would be out of a job and in his place would sit another man who, presumably, would toe the Long line with more loyalty.

Within just a few months after the election, Huey Long had indeed built a new political machine. Although his methods were crude and ruthless, many of his supporters claimed that they were necessary if change were to come to Louisiana. The Old Regulars and other Bourbon Democrats had held the reigns of power tightly for decades; it was perfectly under-standable that Huey had to use extraordinary means to take control. Without resorting to such measures, it is unlikely that he would have been able to gain political office or push through his program of change. As Harvey Peletier, a legislator from Lafourche Parish, remarked, "In my opinion . . . he didn't go nearly as far as they did. In other words, he didn't go nearly as far to get in as they went to keep him out."

Huey Long had made promises to the people of Louisiana, and they were promises he intended to keep. He would concen-trate much of his political energy on fulfilling two of his most popular campaign pledges: to provide all Louisiana school children with free schoolbooks and to build more and better roads in communities throughout the state. With men loyal to Long heading important legislative committees and govern-ment agencies, Huey's programs stood a good chance of passing into law.

The Long administration faced one major obstacle, however: money. In the past, the Louisiana government had steered clear of investing money in the state's infrastructure, and consequently the people of Louisiana paid very little in taxes to the government. When Huey took office, the revenues from taxes were simply not large enough to construct many roads or to improve the schools.

Furthermore, past administrations had shied away from what we now call "deficit spending." The 1921 Constitution prohibited the state from raising money for projects by issuing bonds, interest-bearing certificates sold to citizens by the gov-ernment in order to raise ready cash. Bonds were, in essence, loans: They could be redeemed for a sum larger than the original price at a later date, which meant that the state would be, in effect, borrowing cash from its citizens. Such government financing, still practiced today, is called deficit financing. It allowed states to pay for large expenditures—like the building of roads and schools—which state taxes were insufficient to meet. Louisiana was one of a very few states that did not practice deficit financing in 1928.

With customary vigor, Huey Long set about changing this rule, amending the constitution so he could raise money through a bond issue. In order to make sure that the state had enough money to redeem the bonds when they came due, Huey also proposed an increase in the tax on gasoline, from 2¢ to 4¢ a gallon.

Although Long controlled a bare majority of senators and representatives, passage of a constitutional amendment required the votes of two-thirds of the legislature. Huey and his deputies, Bozeman and Allen, had to work extra hard to convince enough lawmakers to vote for the bill. Some legislators were offered lucrative jobs in state agencies for themselves or promised projects that would bring jobs and benefits to their parishes. Still others later claimed that Long blackmailed them by threatening to reveal family secrets or personal peccadilloes. In July, the amendment and the gasoline tax were passed by the legislature. To become law, however, the amendment required the approval of a majority of Louisiana voters; a referendum would be held in the fall.

Paying for schoolbooks required an equal amount of backroom wheeling and dealing, and in this case, Huey decided to fight two battles at the same time. To raise money for this project, Huey proposed increasing the severance tax levied on natural resources taken ("severed") from the state. This tax increase would fall most heavily on Huey's oldest and most bitter enemies: Standard Oil and other big oil and gas corporations. Huey was able to convince a majority of legislators that Standard Oil could and should contribute more of its profits to help Louisiana's schoolchildren. The bill passed in early July and textbooks were ordered for delivery by the opening of the school year in September.

Despite Long's achievements during his first few months as governor, he met fierce opposition in the legislature. Specifically, 27 members of the House bitterly opposed their new

After a great deal of wheeling and dealing, Huey Long was able to deliver on his highly publicized promise to provide free schoolbooks to the children of Louisiana. (Louisiana State Library)

governor. Calling themselves the Dynamite Squad, they were led by Cecil Morgan of Caddo Parish and J.Y. Sanders, Jr., the son of one of Huey's oldest political opponents, of East Baton Rouge. During the coming months, these men would slowly but steadily erode Governor Long's support among their fellow legislators.

Therefore, although it appeared that Huey's first legislative session was an unqualified success, his battles had only just begun. During the summer, the oil companies, backed by the Dynamite Squad and other anti-Longites, instituted a suit claiming that the severance tax was unconstitutional. According to the suit, the tax violated the 14th Amendment, which prevents the taking of property without due process of law; the oil companies insisted that Louisiana had no right to any of their profits.

Without the money the tax would raise, schoolbooks could not be purchased. Huey staved off immediate disaster by obtaining loans from New Orleans banks that allowed textbooks to be purchased by the time school opened. But it would be months before the case or the future of the schoolbook bill was settled.

In the meantime, Huey campaigned for the bond issue amendment that would allow road and bridge construction to begin. He took to the campaign trail with customary energy and commitment, relishing the chance to reintroduce himself to the people of the state. It was the people and not the politicians, after all, who formed the basis of Huey Long's power and popularity in Louisiana.

One New Orleans attorney and Long supporter, Francis Burns, accompanied Huey on many campaign trips during this period and witnessed the effect the governor had on his constituents. He later described his experiences to a journalist:

> The people I met on those trips—poor, I never saw such poverty—the woman with their teeth so full of tartar they looked like coral shells. They would come to those meetings at night in the cold and the wet with babies wrapped up in blankets and use a flashlight to find their way through the wind . . . Long had given those people hope.

On November 6, 1928, the people of Louisiana ratified the highway bond amendment by an overwhelming majority, giving their new governor the funds he needed to begin road construction and a mandate for his program in general. Children were already attending school, learning from textbooks distributed free by the Long administration.

Storm clouds continued to gather on the horizon, however. Initially won over by promises of jobs and power, many politicians were now beginning to realize the magnitude of Huey's ambition, the ruthlessness with which he pursued his goals, and most importantly, the overwhelming support he commanded among the people of Louisiana. What they realized frightened them; it meant that Huey Long was not a wild upstart, but rather a powerful, enduring force for change.

In addition, Huey Long's methods and manners had begun to arouse the dismay of more and more people in Baton Rouge. His habit of storming into legislative chambers to lobby aggressively for bills he favored shocked the more traditional politicians. Indeed, Huey was often seen haranguing legislators until they agreed to vote for his bills.

Another strike against the new governor was his increasingly sour relationship with the press. Although a truce of sorts had taken place between journalists and the candidate during the gubernatorial campaign, reporters now resumed their critical stance. Huey, who referred to the media as the "lying press," often insulted and threatened individual reporters as well as their employers.

The Long administration also had unique bookkeeping and spending practices: All money taken in or spent by the Long organization was handled by Seymour Weiss, who kept an untold amount of cash in a safe in the Roosevelt Hotel. Funds officially provided by the state for the governor's expenses apparently co-mingled with money donated by constituents directly to the Long organization. Since most of Huey's expenses were paid for in cash and receipts were rarely kept, anti-Long legislators were convinced that Huey was using state money illegally, for personal and political reasons. That he purchased a brand new red Buick automobile and entertained lavishly only increased their suspicions.

Another cause for alarm, even among Long's most ardent supporters, was the new governor's spirit of revenge and retribution. Any perceived slight could provoke Huey's anger, and outright dissent could lead to devastating results. Cecil Morgan, leader of the Dynamite Squad from Caddo Parish, announced that his parish would not accept the free schoolbooks offered by the Long administration; Caddo parents would not accept charity, claimed Morgan, nor did the largely Protestant citizens accept the fact that Catholic schools would be receiving free schoolbooks, too.

Huey struck back by threatening to withhold a major project, a federal army air base, from being built in Shreveport, the parish's seat. If the people of Caddo wanted the airbase, they must accept the schoolbooks and, in addition, the Caddo delegation in the legislature would have to announce that it was going to support the governor's program in the upcoming special session of the legislature. Anxious for the millions of dollars and hundreds of jobs the airbase would bring to their community, the people of Caddo—and Cecil Morgan—backed down and agreed to distribute Huey's schoolbooks. "I didn't coerce them. I stomped them into distributing the books," he said.

Huey Long could hold onto grudges for longer than most politicians. A year later, when a delegation from Caddo Parish came to Baton Rouge to request financial aid for road construction, Huey launched into a bitter tirade, threatening to withhold funding until the parish "humbled" itself. "I will teach you to get off the sidewalk, take off your hat, and bow down damn low when Governor Long comes to town."

Even with his supporters, Huey could be rude and cruel. House member Fred Blanche remembers an incident between Huey and Jess Nugent, a member of the Highway Commission, that took place during a meeting held in the first legislative session. "While Huey was talking, Jess would say at intervals, 'I think . . .' Finally, Huey snapped. 'Goddamn you, shut up. If you could think, I wouldn't have put you on the commission. You're not supposed to think.'"

In early 1929, Huey Long felt confident enough in his political victories to break ties with three of his closest colleagues: Paul Cyr, his lieutenant governor, John Sullivan of the New Regulars, and Colonel Ewing, who owned the New Orleans *States* newspaper. The reasons Huey severed each relationship were complicated, but in the end they had less to do with any specific problem than in one simple fact: Huey Long disliked being told what to do, and these three men felt that they had the right to give Huey advice and to expect him to follow it.

It was a crucial mistake. Huey was cutting off support just when he would need it most. In February 1929, the severance tax bill was declared unconstitutional according to the 14th Amendment by the United States Supreme Court; such action was taken primarily to hinder popular state leaders, like Huey Long, in their efforts to tax the profits of big corporations. Huey would not be able to raise the money needed to pay for free schoolbooks that year, or any year, in this manner. He quickly drew up another plan, one that involved revising the severance tax and imposing an additional tax of 5¢ per barrel on refined oil. He called for a special session of the legislature to meet for six days, beginning March 18, in order to enact the legislation.

When Standard Oil and other corporations got wind of Huey's plan to impose yet another tax on their profits, they joined anti-Long members of the legislature in demanding that the governor be stopped. This time, Huey Long had gone too far. The Louisiana economy, for better or worse, depended on corporations like Standard Oil, and Huey appeared bound and determined to make them pay a price for doing business in the state. The proposed oil tax galvanized Long's opponents and destroyed the legislative majority he had created the year before.

Sensing that he was about to lose the fight, Huey arranged to have this special session adjourned after just three days. He called for a new session, one that would meet for 18 days, in hopes that with enough time he could regain lost ground. The extra time, however, only gave the opposition more opportunities to develop a strategy to bring the governor down. Again, Huey called for an adjournment.

His plan failed utterly. On Monday, March 15, 1929, Speaker of the House John Fournet called for adjournment only to be met with a protest from Huey's archenemy, Cecil Morgan. Morgan shouted out that he had in his hand an affidavit describing a remarkable accusation against the governor: Huey Long, claimed a citizen of Baton Rouge, had tried to procure the assassination of a member of the House of Representatives, one J. Y. Sanders. Furthermore, on the desk of every representative was a copy of a petition citing 19 charges of impeachment against Governor Long.

Within moments of Morgan's statement, the House chamber erupted in confusion. Fournet quickly called for a vote to adjourn and members of the House began to cast their ballots. Then, an unfortunate incident occurred: The electronic voting machine jammed, and it appeared that only 13 members—well below the number of known anti-Longites—were against adjournment. A virtual riot broke out among the representatives gathered in the House chamber, complete with fist fights and overturned chairs. From then on, March 25, 1929 was known as Bloody Monday in Louisiana.

The impeachment charges against Huey Long ranged from the absurd to the reasonable. The attempted murder charge was certainly untrue and was eventually dropped, as were several others, including "engagement in immoral and illegal activities in nightclubs" and "uttering blasphemous and sacrilegious expressions." The House heard testimony until April 25, more than two weeks after the official close of the special session on April 6. When the House finally adjourned, it presented eight charges of impeachment to the Senate; if a two-thirds of the Senate members found just one of the charges to be true, Huey would be removed from office.

The impeachment articles accused Huey Long of bribing legislators, misappropriating state funds, and seeking to intimidate the press. The last charge referred to a case involving Charles Manship, the publisher of the Baton Rouge *Morning Advocate* and *State Times*, who had come out strongly against the new taxes. Apparently, Huey had threatened to reveal that Manship's brother was a mental patient at East Louisiana State Hospital if Manship continued to thwart him. Although Huey admitted making the threat, he claimed he did so only to show how hypocritical Manship was being in refusing to support taxes meant to improve an institution serving one of his own family members.

Article VIII of the impeachment bill was a blanket charge against the governor, claiming "incompetency, corruption, and gross misconduct." The undated letters of resignation he forced his officials to sign, his appearance in the House and Senate chambers during votes, and providing jobs to relatives were among the deeds enveloped by Article VIII.

Was Huey Long guilty of the charges brought by the Louisiana House of Representatives? Without question, Huey's use of patronage and his loose spending practices would be considered highly unethical, if not illegal. But it was equally clear that politicians in Louisiana had been using the same techniques for decades, if not as skillfully at least as often as Huey Long. His supporters brought up these points often during the House proceedings, but to no avail. The House presented the charges to the Senate, which arranged to meet on May 15 to begin the impeachment trial.

Tensions ran high in the capital as Huey waited to face the Senate hearing. Harley Bozeman, O. K. Allen, Seymour Weiss, and Huey's brother Earl Long were the only men he felt he could trust. Each of them did their best to rally support for the governor, who appeared seriously shaken by the events. "They've got me," Huey said to an aide, who found the governor in tears one evening during the House hearings.

At one point, even his oldest friend, Harley Bozeman, had doubts that Huey could pull through. Late one night, he came to Huey's suite at the Heidelberg Hotel and advised him to resign. "Huey was sitting there, paring his toenails," Bozeman later recalled, "He had just trimmed off the big toe, looked at the piece of nail on the floor and said, 'I wouldn't give the value of that toenail for a son of a bitch like you.'" Bozeman later resigned his important committee chairmanship and the relationship between the two old friends was never repaired.

Huey Long was stopped only momentarily, however. He soon shook off his despair and rallied his energy. Borrowing about $40,000 from Robert Maestri, a supporter and wealthy New Orleans businessman, he waged a campaign to restore his good name among the people that mattered most: the citizens of Louisiana. He did so not by answering the charges brought against him, but by changing the field of battle altogether. He was being impeached, Long claimed, because he had threatened Standard Oil and the legislators who worked for them. One circular distributed stated his defense in this way:

> I had rather go down to a thousand impeachments than to admit that I am the Governor of the State that does not dare to call the Standard Oil Company to account so that we can educate our children and care for the destitute, sick, and afflicted.

In the end, however, it was not Huey's appeals to the people that saved his political career. Instead, he devised another brilliant maneuver that in effect stopped the Senate hearings before they could begin. Huey convinced 16 senators—with the usual promises of jobs and power—to sign a bill called a Round Robin. The Round Robin stated that because only one of the charges had been passed during the official session of the House that ended on April 6, the other charges were invalid. The senators claimed that they would not vote for impeachment on these charges no matter what the evidence presented showed. In addition, the charge made by Charles Manship was also invalid because it was, in essence, a private situation between Long and Manship.

When the bill was shown to members of the legislature, they had no choice but to adjourn the session without a vote since they would fail to garner the two-thirds majority necessary to impeach the governor. When Huey Long agreed to shelve the offending taxes on oil corporations, the businessmen agreed to urge their state senators to vote to dismiss the bills of impeachment at the next regular legislative session the following year.

Huey Long had managed to stave off a serious threat to his administration. Although he had suffered a clear defeat at the hands of the state's powerful business interests, and despite the serious charges of bribery and misappropriation of funds, the voters of the state appeared to be behind him. He knew, too, that between his threats and his promises, he could regain control of the legislature before it met again the following May.

Nevertheless, his friends and associates saw a change in Huey, one that they believed might spell his ultimate downfall. "Impeachment did something to him," said Leonard Spark, a pro-Long member of the legislature. "It made him vicious. After that, he fought his enemies with everything he had and gave his friends everything he had."

8

THE REIGN OF THE KINGFISH
Governor of Louisiana: 1929–1931

> "I don't argue with 'em, I just stomp hell out of 'em.
>
> —*Huey P. Long*

Although Huey Long emerged from his impeachment fight with the governorship intact, he knew his victory was a shallow one. Only a clever sleight-of-hand had staved off disaster; Long still faced major opposition within and outside the government. Among his most bitter enemies were his own lieutenant governor, Paul Cyr, the chief justice of the state supreme court, and the state attorney general. Nearly all of Louisiana's newspapers had called for his removal from office during the impeachment hearings. Most importantly, Huey Long knew that 7 of the 18 impeachment charges could be brought up again at the next legislative session the following May. He had less than a year to shore up support.

In the meantime, his opposition reorganized quickly. On June 12, 1929, the headline of the New Orleans *States Times,* read, "Parker Heads League to Save State from Long." Former Governor John Parker and some 300 politicians, business leaders, and corporation lawyers met in a New Orleans hotel to form the Constitutional League, an organization to "keep Long from treating the organic law like a scrap of paper." Within 15 minutes, the group raised $100,000 to fund continued investigations into corruption in the Long administration. The league's goal was to revive impeachment charges at the next session, and replace Speaker of the House John Fournet for his role in the events of Bloody Monday.

With a characteristic display of bravado, Huey dismissed his opposition as the "Constipation League" and the "League of Notions." He also struck back hard and fast. First, he rewarded his supporters, particularly the Round Robin signers, with state jobs and powerful political positions. He also began a campaign to force from the state boards men who either had not stood by him in the recent crisis or might not do so in the future. He forced the president of the Levee Board to resign his post and gained control of the Orleans Dock Board by forcing out the one member who had kept him from having a dependable majority.

He struck with equal vigor at members of congress who had tried to impeach him. Using House Speaker John Fournet and the newly elected president pro tempore of the Senate, Alvin O. King, Huey purged important committees of anti-Long legislators. He also initiated recall movements against nine legislators, based on generally specious charges, hoping to remove them entirely from their offices.

To friends and enemies alike, Huey Long was even more high strung and less patient than he had been in the past; his new nickname was "Your Truculency." In addition, the governor's fear of being attacked or assassinated had reached a new high. He was well aware that his actions upset powerful people with crucial interests to protect, and not all of them were averse to violence. "Sure, I carry a gun," he told a reporter. "Sometimes I carry four. You never know when someone's going to shoot at the Kingfish." He added several men to his bodyguard staff, men who followed him everywhere he went.

Despite his generally combative frame of mind, Huey was astute enough to recognize an important opportunity for compromise. In July 1929, he and Harvey Couch, a powerful businessman and organizer of a new "citizen's committee" announced a truce between the Long administration and some of Louisiana's more powerful business interests. Couch and his colleagues, concluding that the present state of political turmoil was damaging Louisiana's potential for economic development, made Huey an attractive offer.

If Huey would retract the recall proceedings against anti-Long legislators and promise not to institute a severance tax—the threatened tax that had brought on the impeachment effort in the first place—the committee would use its influence not only to discourage attempts to renew the impeachment charges, but also to marshal support for Huey's legislative program. The next day, Couch's group proved their influence when the Standard Oil Company announced that it would no longer oppose the severance tax and that it would expand its Baton Rouge refinery. The unique truce between Huey and Louisiana's business world took much of Louisiana by surprise.

During the summer and fall, Huey continued to prepare for the next legislative session, which would take place in May 1930. In speeches and public statements throughout the state, Huey outlined his plans. No doubt he upset many of his newly acquired supporters by outlining far more ambitious proposals than expected. "We propose to go faster," Huey remarked as he unveiled his plans to call for an additional 3¢ gasoline tax and a $68 million highway bond. He also planned to recommend legislation to restore New Orleans to its former position as a great port, including a bill to retire the port's debts and one to construct a free bridge across the Mississippi River.

The proposal that attracted the most attention and controversy was Huey's idea for a new state capitol. At a cost of $5 million, the skyscraper Huey envisioned would be the tallest state capitol building in the country. Although few people doubted that the old Louisiana State Capitol was woefully inadequate to meet the needs of a rapidly expanding economy and government, Huey's extravagant plan was seen as a needlessly expensive monument to his own ego.

Indeed, the plan for the new capitol building followed directly on the heels of another building project that had outraged much of Louisiana during the previous winter. Despite widespread objections, Huey Long had torn down the governor's mansion he loathed and begun construction on a new one, having manipulated the legislature into providing him with funds and using state convicts to perform some of the labor.

During construction of the mansion, which continued until the following May, Huey continued to reside in a suite in the Heidelburg Hotel while in Baton Rouge and the Roosevelt Hotel whenever he visited New Orleans. Rose and the children remained at the family home in Shreveport, leaving the governor to indulge his fondness for good food and, often, too much liquor. Although his family would move into the new mansion with him, Rose appeared unable to keep her husband from

Although the Long family was rarely seen in Baton Rouge, Russell Long, Huey's second child, spent some time with his father. Russell would later follow in Huey's political footsteps, serving a 37-year tenure in the United States Senate. (Louisiana State Library)

drinking too much; "I've been under the influence of liquor more nights of my adult life than I've been sober," admitted Huey, "and out of this have come some of the most brilliant ideas of my career." Nevertheless, his often public displays of overindulgence did nothing to win over his more conservative constituents.

In fact, excess of any kind appeared out of place in Louisiana, across the country, and throughout much of the Western world during the winter of 1929–30. The public was still reeling from the shock of the stock market crash that took place on October 29, 1929. Precipitated by hectic stock speculation, lowered foreign trade, and overproduction of agricultural products, the crash heralded a period of high unemployment, failing businesses and banks, and plummeting agricultural prices. In the United States alone, more than 16 million people lost their jobs within three years. The effects of the Depression would endure for almost a decade.

According to a 1969 essay in *Louisiana History* magazine, however, "New York could have been a million miles away" from Louisiana in the fall of 1929, perhaps because the state had much less far to fall than more prosperous regions of the country. Indeed, the average income of Louisiana families amounted to less than half the national average—both before and after the crash. In rural areas, people had always been subjected to the vagaries of nature and, in the cities, industry had never offered many permanent jobs.

At first, it seemed that the Great Depression would have little effect on the state. A few days after the New Year, however, a prominent citizen, the president and treasurer of the New Orleans Baseball and Amusement Company, shot himself to death, his suicide taking place in the grandstands of the ballpark he owned and loved. Some say it was his health, others the $300,000 he had lost in the crash.

This jolting event was a harbinger of things to come: Within three years, Louisiana's per capita income would decline from $415 to $222 and farm income would fall from $170 million to $59 million. As the years passed, conditions in this already poor state would continue to worsen, making the already difficult lives of most Louisianians even more onerous.

In some ways, the onset of the Depression probably helped Huey Long. The jobs he offered as patronage and those that resulted from his ever-expanding public works program were even more highly valued as private businesses continued to fail throughout the state. Even more importantly, his popularity with a beleaguered citizenry grew with every road he paved and every schoolbook he distributed. For many, these were the only tangible signs of hope in sight. It was also true that his response to the financial crisis—bolstering the Louisiana economy by adding public works programs and infusing the treasury with an influx of capital by selling state bonds—was economically sound, if not entirely successful.

Despite Huey's overtures to the conservative elements in Louisiana, the May 1930 legislative session was a stormy one. Much to Huey's dismay, the Old Regulars remained hostile to his administration. With its 19-member delegation, it was able to prevent a two-thirds majority vote in favor of Huey's legislation. The legislature adjourned in July without enacting a single major Long bill.

Huey Long's first reaction was a typical one. He struck hard and fast at the city that had thwarted him, pressuring New Orleans banks to stop lending money to the city, forcing New Orleans to borrow from New York banks. Then, on July 15, he made a startling announcement: He would run for the United States Senate in the fall. If he won, he would take his victory to mean that the voters supported his program; in fact, his campaign slogan would be "Complete the Work." If he lost, he would resign as governor, leaving the state in the hands of his opposition.

Huey Long made another remarkable promise to his constituents. Even if he won election to the Senate, he would serve out the year and a half left of his gubernatorial term. This time would allow him to choose and install his replacement, a governor who, unlike Lieutenant Governor Paul Cyr, would follow the Long program. When asked about the propriety of leaving a U.S. Senate seat empty for so long, Huey replied that it had been virtually vacant ever since the incumbent—his opponent—had assumed the seat nearly twenty years before.

The incumbent in question, Joseph Ransdell, was a conservative politician from northeastern Louisiana. Born in 1858 on a plantation, he had been educated in New York and had practiced law before serving two terms in the House of Representatives. He was first elected to the United States Senate in 1912 and had held his seat ever since. Tall, gray-haired, and with a fluffy moustache and goatee, Senator Ransdell was the very picture of an old-time Southern patriarch, and a perfect foil for the Kingfish's vitriolic tongue. In speech after speech,

Huey referred to his opponent as "Old Feather Duster" in reference to his bushy facial hair.

Huey's campaign for the Senate was as unconventional as any of his others. Investing about $60,000 in sound trucks, he became one of the first politicians to use this technique, rolling into towns with speakers blaring out his message. He organized crews of advance men to drum up crowds with music. State prisoners even painted Huey's face on tire covers.

Despite the fact that he was running for a national office, Huey continued to speak almost exclusively on state matters. He extolled the present and future benefits of his highway construction program, continued to condemn the influence of corporate interests on government, and made many promises about the direction he would take the state in the future. In a moment of open frankness that September, he told a reporter from the Baton Rouge *State Times,* "When I lie from the stump, I lie big, because no matter what the newspapers say, 90 percent of the people will believe me."

Just to make sure that his message was communicated to as much of the population as possible, Huey began his own newspaper. Called the *Louisiana Progress,* it was "the most cheerfully venomous regular publication in the nation," according to Harnett Kane, a contemporary journalist in Louisiana. Huey hired a reporter formerly associated with the *Times-Picayune* and a free-lance cartoonist with a penchant for caricature. Although the paper included sections on the arts and society, and a full sports section, Huey's accomplishments and his enemies' shortcomings were highlighted throughout.

One early issue included an eight-column map of Louisiana showing highways Long would build if he won the election; the *Progress* claimed that the highway work "will be the greatest single step ever taken in the United States for state improvement." The publication was also filled with characteristic invective. An article in one of its first issues described Ransdell as "senile and ineffective."

Thoroughly partisan, the *Progress* claimed a circulation of about 125,000, larger than that of any Louisiana daily. Part, if not most, of its success was due to Huey's dubious marketing techniques: He compelled every state employee to order from 10 to 15 subscriptions apiece. Furthermore, firms seeking state contracts were urged to purchase advertising in the publication as well as order a healthy number of subscriptions to distribute to its employees.

At about this time, Huey Long began a new and equally dubious system of raising revenue to fund his newspaper, his Senate campaign, and other activities of the Long machine. This system, known as "deducts," consisted of obligatory deductions from the salaries of all state employees. Beginning in August 1930, the amount of deducts ranged from 2 to 22% percent of a state employee's salary, depending on how much he earned and the position he held; the higher the salary and position, the more "deducts" he contributed.

Surprisingly little complaint was heard about this highly unethical, if not illegal, practice. Most people apparently thought that the deducts were a small price to pay for receiving relatively high-paying state jobs. In addition, it appeared that Huey could be flexible on the matter: One supporter reported that "If a man couldn't afford to pay his full amount of deducts, he could go to Huey and say, 'I got sickness in the family,' 'I got a boy in college' and Huey would say, 'All right, don't bother.'" During Christmas, Easter, and other holidays, the deducts were alleviated to add cash to the pockets of workers at a time when it would be especially appreciated. Soon, the Long organization was financially self-sufficient.

In the meantime, Huey's summer campaign for the U.S. Senate was going strong. As Huey toured his state, he capitalized on perhaps his greatest asset: his ability to communicate with the people on their level. Unlike those of his opponent, Huey's voice, face, and principles were known throughout the state. Indeed, the challenge Huey offered at nearly ever campaign stop was: "How many people here know the names of your U.S. Senators? Well, when I get to Washington, you'll surely know who's representing you."

With plenty of money and his own characteristic energy as resources, Huey ran a nearly flawless campaign. Just before the election, however, a scandal erupted that had the potential of sinking his candidacy, if not his entire political career. Two men, James Terrell and Sam Irby, the ex-husband and uncle of Huey's mistress, Alice Lee Grosjean, threatened to expose the Kingfish's love affair to the public. In addition, Irby, who had been fired from the Highway Commission for incompetence, promised to reveal corruption within that commission to Huey's enemy, the state attorney general.

The two men arrived at a Shreveport hotel and, foolishly, told Grosjean of their intentions. Within hours, state police arrived to take the two men into custody for "questioning." For several days, Irby and Terrell seemed to disappear without a trace. When journalists found out about what appeared to be a kidnapping, the story became front-page news. The governor, however, treated the matter alternately as a joke and as a mystery to him, until he was threatened with habeus corpus proceedings by the state attorney general.

On the Sunday before the Tuesday election, Huey went on the radio from his hotel room. He produced a man he called Sam Irby, who claimed he himself had asked to be taken into protective custody. The matter was summarily dropped and Louisiana citizens, presumably laughing all the way to the polls, voted for the Kingfish in record numbers.

Long easily defeated Ransdell, polling 149,640 votes to Ransdell's 111,451. As usual, Long won by a huge majority in the rural parishes, and, surprisingly, polled his largest number of voters in New Orleans yet, losing by less than 4,000. Facing no opposition in the general election, Long became a senator-elect at the age of 37.

Huey Long's victory truly made him the Kingfish of Louisiana. Indeed, he enthusiastically proclaimed, "I ain't no fish! I'm gonna pick another name, maybe one with a lion or a tiger in it." On September 16, just a week after the senatorial election, Long called to order a special session of the legislature. Every one of his major proposals passed into law. Of the 100 legislators in the House, only 21 opposed any part of his program; only 6 of the 39 senators were still anti-Long. Even the Old Regulars surrendered, agreeing to halt a revival of the impeachment charges and offering support for most of his legislative program. Funds to build the new skyscraper capitol were offered as well and construction began immediately.

For the next year and a half, Long kept his promise to the people of Louisiana by refusing to leave the state in the hands of his lieutenant governor "even for one minute." At times, the power struggle between Long and Cyr rose to comic heights. In October 1931, Cyr went so far as to visit a justice of the peace and took the oath of office as governor, declaring that Huey had vacated the office as soon as he was chosen U.S. Senator. In a dramatic play, for he was in no real danger of being displaced by Cyr's attempted coup d'etat, Huey called out the National Guard, the state police, and the highway police. Motorized troops circled the governor's mansion and the governor's office "to prevent Cyr from seizing them," as one story in the *Times-Picayune* retold.

Then Huey turned the tables. By taking the oath of office as governor, Huey claimed, Cyr had vacated his *own* office. Alvin O. King, the pro-Long president of the Senate, took over as lieutenant governor as next in line for the job. Huey remarked to a reporter, "[Cyr] is no longer lieutenant governor, and he is now nothing." To add insult to injury, countless people across the state, some probably encouraged by the Long organization, mocked Cyr's action by coming before notary publics to take the oath as Louisiana governor.

With state power firmly in his hands in the fall of 1930, Huey turned his attention toward a state institution he had so far ignored: Louisiana State University (LSU). Located a few miles south of Baton Rouge, LSU enrolled about 1,800 students (all white in this segregated state), employed just 168 professors, and had an operating budget of under $800,000 when Huey took office in 1928. In the rating of schools maintained by the intercollegiate Associations of State Universities, LSU was on the "C" list, or third rate.

When LSU's president, Thomas Atkinson, suffered a heart attack in 1930, Huey Long looked at the vacancy left by his impending resignation as a chance to make LSU "my university." From then on, he was intimately involved in university affairs, appropriating money for its expansion, attending its athletic events, and overseeing the hiring and firing of faculty.

His first appointment made Dr. James Monroe Smith, a professor with a doctorate from Columbia University, LSU's new president. Although Smith was a competent academic, he was clearly hired because Long felt he could control him. "There's not a straight bone in Jim Smith's body," Huey later admitted, "but he does what I want him to, so I think he's a good president."

Using funds collected through the severance tax and others diverted from the Highway Commission's budget, Long quickly made his mark on the university. He enlarged the campus, adding a music and dramatic arts building, women's dormitories, and a fine arts building, among other structures. By 1935, LSU would double its all-white student body, attract renowned professors from across the country, and earn an "A" rating from the national accrediting institution.

Perhaps because he never had attended college himself, Huey seemed quite drawn to the university's extracurricular trappings. He especially loved the football team, the LSU Tigers, and attended nearly every game and every practice. As usual, Huey put in his two cents whenever the mood struck him, without regard either for his position or for the rules of the game. He constantly harassed coaches and players who did not perform to his rigorous standards. During one game, he took exception to the way one referee conducted himself. Marching out onto the field, he pointed his finger at the surprised official and said, "I'm Governor Long. If you want to penalize my boys do it out in the middle of the field, not near the goal line."

Perhaps his greatest contribution to the university was the creation of a new medical school, the second in the state's history. One of the reasons for the state's failure to provide adequate medical care to its people, Huey reasoned, was its lack of doctors. In early December 1930, he announced that LSU would establish a medical school in New Orleans. The new medical school would offer students a less expensive alternative to the state's only other medical school, the overcrowded Tulane University College of Medicine. A physician and member of the Tulane faculty admitted to being surprised by Huey's understanding of the issues involved, later recalling, "I was utterly astonished by his knowledge of medical history and what was needed to make a good medical school."

Huey's interest in education went beyond the walls of LSU. He also raised money through a series of tax measures to improve public schools throughout the state; by 1935 the state pledged $10 million into the school fund, twice the amount of state support in 1928. Perhaps most extraordinary were Huey Long's efforts to improve the adult literacy rates. Once again diverting tax money from other programs, he established a number of night schools to educate illiterate Louisianians. Over 100,000 people, both black and white, attended.

In 1934, he spoke of his intentions in the *Progress*. "We started them to school. They learned to read. They learned to work simple arithmetic problems. Now some of our plantation owners can't figure the poor devils out of everything at the close of the year."

As involved as he was in the affairs of his state, Huey Long would not remain a purely local phenomenon for much longer. Two rather silly incidents brought him his most widespread national publicity to date. The first occured in March 1930 when a German cruiser called the *Emden* arrived in New Orleans. Its commander, Lothar von Arnauld de la Perière, paid a courtesy call on the governor and senator-elect of Louisiana in his suite at the Roosevelt Hotel. Much to his dismay, he found the Kingfish dressed in green silk pajamas, a red and blue lounging robe, and blue bedroom slippers. (One of the reporters wrote that the governor looked like "an explosion in a paint factory.")

Although Huey's friends and enemies alike had long ago accepted his unconventional habits, the German commander was horrified and demanded an official apology. "My country has been insulted," the commander told Seymour Weiss, "I demand an apology." Although Huey refused to issue an official apology, he made amends by visiting the consul the next day in proper dress, with a "collar so high I had to stand on a stool to spit over it."

The green pajamas affair drew wide comment in the national and foreign press. Some thought it was a publicity stunt, but those closest to Huey saw the act for what it was, an attempt to show that Huey Long was indeed the Kingfish, powerful enough to receive anyone, including a foreign ambassador, on his own terms.

The second incident occurred almost a year later. For three weeks, newspapers from Boston to New Orleans to Washington were caught up in a controversy over the proper way to eat cornpone (a kind of cornbread "hard enough to knock down a yearling") and potlikker (the juice from boiled vegetable greens and salt pork fat). According to Huey Long, who spoke of the virtues of potlikker in countless interviews with reporters, the proper way to consume his favorite dish was to first dunk the cornpone into the potlikker then bite off a piece.

Julian Harris, the witty editor of the Atlanta *Constitution,* took exception with Huey's method, claiming that only by crumbling the cornpone into the potlikker and then eating the dish with a spoon could the Southern delicacy be truly appreciated. On February 17, 1931 the *Constitution* wrote "The battle line is drawn . . . and once more there will be waged a fight on a real American issue in which prohibition will pale before a question that is genuinely fundamental." Indeed, people from all over the country lined up on one side or the other. Even Franklin Delano Roosevelt, future president of the United States, had an opinion: "I must admit that I crumble mine."

Later, Long told Julian Harris that the controversy was the "only delightful pastime" he had had since becoming governor. No doubt readers of the *Constitution* and other newspapers, weary as they were from the hardships of the Depression, were also grateful for the amusing diversion.

Without doubt, Huey enjoyed gaining the public spotlight, no matter what the reason, but he had more than fun on his mind as he prepared to take his Senate seat. By the summer of 1931, the Depression had exacted a heavy toll on agricultural prices, especially in the South. Huey proposed a "cotton holiday": In 1932, no Southern state would plant cotton, thereby increasing demand—and the price—for the commodity. He invited the governors and other officials of seven southern states to a meeting to discuss the proposal on August 21.

A majority of those who attended were willing to consider the plan, at least tentatively—if Louisiana passed the first prohibitory law and only if the plan was adopted by states producing three-fourths of the total cotton supply. At Huey's urging, the Louisiana legislature, meeting in special session, enacted a 1932 moratorium on cotton planting within two weeks. Nevertheless, the fate of the cotton holiday rested with Texas, the largest cotton producer in the country. When Texas refused to endorse the plan, Huey called its governor a "dirty millionaire" and accused the Texas legislature of being "blandished with wine, women, and money . . . paid off like a slot machine." Huey's novel plan was dead in the water.

Huey Long would have greater success in his own state later that fall when the election campaign to elect his successor finally began. Huey's choice for governor was his old friend,

Oscar K. Allen, who had served as Highway Commissioner since 1928. Silver-haired and soft-spoken, Allen was known more for his loyalty to Huey Long than for his personal strength or intelligence. But the other candidates—George Guion, a respected New Orleans lawyer, and Dudley LeBlanc, member of the Public Service Commission—were well aware that they would be running against Huey Long, not O. K. Allen, and it would be an uphill race.

The election held on January 19, 1932 proved that the people of Louisiana still believed in their beloved Kingfish. Allen won by more than 100,000 votes over LeBlanc and by about 150,000 over Guion. Huey Long's dominion over his home state was indeed secure. However, although Allen's ascension to governor cemented Huey's relationship to the people of the state, it nearly destroyed his relationship with his family. For Earl Long, Huey's ambitious younger brother, had lobbied hard to become Allen's running mate as lieutenant governor. Huey refused him, choosing instead John Fournet, former Speaker of the House.

Huey did so for at least two reasons: First, he knew it was political suicide to run two men from the same part of the state—indeed, the very same town—on the same ticket. Second, and most importantly, he knew that Earl would dominate the more passive Allen when Huey was in Washington and thus "the wrong Long would be running the state," as historian T. Harry Williams put it.

Finally, Huey felt he could leave Louisiana without losing his power or influence over the state. On January 20, he traveled by private car to Washington, accompanied by his wife, Rose, Seymour Weiss, Mayor Walmsey, and Governor-elect Allen. Another car was filled with other cronies, all of whom had come to see the Kingfish sworn in as senator. "I'm leaving state politics for good," Huey told a reporter. "I've done all I can for Louisiana. Now I want to help the rest of the country."

9

TERROR OF THE BAYOUS
Huey Long, U.S. Senator: 1932–1935

> "A mob is coming here . . . to hang you damned scoundrels and I'm undecided whether to stick with you or go out and lead them."
>
> —*Huey P. Long to the United States Senate*

The 72nd Congress had been in session for nearly two months when Huey finally arrived for his swearing-in ceremony. Bucking tradition as usual, he presented himself before the Senate without first being introduced by the senior senator from Louisiana, Edward Broussard. He also ignored a regulation against smoking, puffing away on his cigar constantly until it was time to take the oath, then again when he was finished. "Within an hour," wrote a reporter for the New York *Times*, "the 'Terror of the Bayous' . . . was violating every rule of decorum in that august chamber."

As always, however, Huey Long's flamboyant style was offset by political substance. Throughout his term in the Senate, he took every opportunity to address what he saw as the basic challenge faced by the United States: the accumulation of capital in the hands of the few. In one speech in 1931, Long asked and answered the question of what had caused the Depression by saying: "There is but one reason; it is because a handful of men in the United States own all the money in this country."

On April 4, 1931, Long delivered a powerful speech entitled "The Doom of America's Dream." He did so partially in response to a message sent to the Senate from President Herbert Hoover requesting that Congress consider proposing a bill to balance the federal budget. In the 30-minute speech, Long challenged Hoover and his own Democratic colleagues to reconsider their priorities; a balanced budget would mean nothing to someone who could not afford to feed his family. According to Long, the very principles upon which this country was founded were at risk:

> The great and grand dream of America that all men are created free and equal, endowed with the inalienable right of life and liberty and the pursuit of happiness—this great dream of America, this light and this great hope—has almost gone out of sight in this day and time, and everybody knows it; and there is a mere candle flicker here and yonder to take the place of what this great dream of America was supposed to be.

The poetic cadence of the speech impressed the correspondents who covered the event, but so did its remarkable content, especially Huey's proposal to redistribute wealth by taxation. A reporter for the Baltimore *Sun* wrote that "no such stirring plea for the impoverished masses has been made in the Senate for years."

This powerful speech established Long as a leading member of the progressive bloc in the Senate, which included among others two Republicans, George Norris of Nebraska and Robert La Follette, Jr. of Wisconsin, as well as fellow Democrat Burton Wheeler of Montana. Huey's rhetoric did not, however, endear him to the Democratic leadership or the more conservative members of either party. Pat Harrison of Mississippi "hated Huey like no one was hated in the Senate"; Virginia's Carter Glass said that Huey was "an unfit associate for any company of gentlemen"; and Harry Byrd of Virginia went so far as to ask to be assigned a new seat away from Huey "even if I have to sit on the Republican side."

Long's relationship with his senatorial colleagues would always be tumultuous. So too would be his association with the national leaders of his own Democratic Party. During the spring of 1932, Huey chose to support Franklin Delano Roosevelt, then governor of New York, in his bid to become the Democratic nominee for president. Born into a wealthy New York family, Roosevelt had been raised in elegant surroundings and educated at Harvard. He had served as an attorney at a New York law firm before being elected state senator and later governor of New York. Although Huey mistrusted Roosevelt's wealth and patrician background, he felt that Roosevelt was the only candidate with any progressive ideas. "I don't like your sonofabitch, but I'll be for him," he told a pro-Roosevelt member of Congress.

On June 27, the Democrats gathered in Chicago to nominate their candidate and Huey Long was there to show his support for Roosevelt. On the final day of the convention, the Roosevelt forces seemed about to collapse after having failed to receive a two-thirds majority in favor of Roosevelt's nomination on three separate ballots. The Roosevelt leaders turned to Huey for help. Using his characteristic combination of reason and intimidation, Huey convinced two wavering Southern states, Arkansas and Mississippi, to remain in the Roosevelt camp. Edward J. Flynn, delegate from New York, later remarked, "There is no question in my mind but that without Long's work, Roosevelt might not have been nominated."

A few weeks after the convention, Huey Long had another chance to exert his growing influence in another political contest: the race for the United States Senate seat in Arkansas. Running against six other candidates was Hattie Carraway, currently serving in the Senate as a replacement for her husband, Senator Thomas Carraway, who had died a year and a half before.

Just two weeks before the election, Arkansas politicos estimated that Carraway would receive no more than 3,000 out of a total of about 250,000 votes. Huey Long decided to help the "little woman" primarily because she had voted with him more often than any of his other colleagues. He also hoped to further spread his name and influence outside of Louisiana.

In a whirlwind campaign that lasted just one week, Huey Long delivered 39 speeches, traveled about 2,000 miles, and addressed approximately 200,000 people. "A cyclone just went through here and is headed your way," one Arkansas politician cautioned another. "Very few trees left standing and even these badly scarred up."

In nearly every speech, Huey warned of the dire fate that awaited the nation if people like Hattie Carraway were driven from office: "If Wall Street and their trust gang succeed in

Huey Long proved his growing national influence when he swept through Arkansas campaigning for Hattie Carraway. With Huey's help, Carraway became the first woman to be elected to a full term in the United States Senate. (Louisiana State Library)

defeating enough senators who have stood with the people like this little woman senator from Arkansas has . . . you'll never be able to get anyone from this state to stand by you again." On election day, the fruits of Long's labor were evident: Hattie won by a popular vote that equaled the total vote of her six opponents combined to become the first woman ever to be elected to a full six-year term to the Senate.

The near-miracle Huey performed in Arkansas impressed the powers-that-be in Washington. When Huey asked to be included in the national campaign to elect Franklin Roosevelt, he could not be denied. In early October, he was invited to lunch at Roosevelt's residence in Hyde Park, New York, ostensibly to discuss Huey's campaign role.

The two men sitting at the luncheon table could not have been more different: Franklin Roosevelt, dignified, highly educated, and elegantly tailored next to pudgy, street-smart Long dressed in a plaid suit, orchid shirt, and pink necktie. What the two spoke of at the luncheon has never been recorded, but observers remarked that Roosevelt seemed captivated by his Southern guest. His mother, Sara Roosevelt, was less impressed. "Who is that *awful* man sitting on my son's right?" she was heard to ask in a loud whisper.

Although Roosevelt and his team continued to consider Long to be a relatively harmless Southern demagogue without much influence outside of his home state, members of the national Democratic leadership recognized Long's growing appeal—and the danger to Roosevelt that it posed. When Huey asked the Democratic National Committee for a special train equipped with loudspeakers in which to tour the country, they did their best to rein him in. Huey spoke in support of Roosevelt (and, as always, on his own behalf) in just four states—North and South Dakota, Nebraska, and Kansas—but everywhere he appeared, he attracted large and enthusiastic crowds. James Farley, director of the Roosevelt campaign and chairman of the Democratic National Committee, later admitted, "We never underrated him again." Roosevelt won the election by a landslide and Huey Long was responsible for a small part of this victory.

For a time, Huey's relationship with Roosevelt appeared to be a solid one. "When I was talking to the Governor today," he told a reporter in October 1932, "I just felt like the Depression was over. That's a fact. I never felt so tickled in my life." Their honeymoon would be a short one, however.

In March, President Roosevelt unveiled his plans to stimulate the economy and bring the Great Depression to an end with a series of legislative acts known as the New Deal. In this legislative session, Democrats in the Senate introduced bills to give the federal government more control over agricultural, corporate, and banking institutions, as well as bills to organize public relief and employment projects. Many Americans were impressed with Roosevelt's dramatic attempts to quell the economic crisis still gripping the nation.

Huey Long, however, objected strongly to almost all New Deal legislation for two main reasons. First, he felt that the New Deal did not go nearly far enough to change the fundamental structure of the economy by decentralizing wealth and power. Second, he felt that the "little man" he had championed throughout his career was not being treated fairly. Instead, Roosevelt's program favored big business over small and rich men over poor. On bill after bill, Huey rose before the Senate to show his colleagues how the measures presented in the New Deal would disappoint the average man, benefit large corporations, and fail to bring about a redistribution of wealth.

Despite Huey's best efforts, the Congress passed the majority of New Deal legislation during this session. Long did not, however, celebrate with his fellow Democrats. "I do not care for my share in a victory that means that the poor and the downtrodden, the blind, the helpless, the orphaned, the bleeding, the wounded, the hungry, and the distressed, will be the victims," he said to his colleagues in the Senate.

Huey's conflict with President Roosevelt did not end with the 1933 legislative session. In fact, it had only just begun. Although the New Deal programs had put thousands of men and women to work, hundreds of thousands more remained poor and without hope. As the Depression headed into its fourth year, more and more Americans were getting impatient with Roosevelt's attempts at solving the crisis. H. G. Wells, British writer and commentator, wrote during a visit to the United States in 1934 that "the actual New Deal has not gone far enough and fast enough for [the American people], and that is what the shouting is about."

In 1934, Huey Long was perhaps the loudest shouter in the country. During a 30-minute radio speech on February 23, Huey announced that he was creating a new organization that would promote his program for redistribution of wealth. Called "Share Our Wealth," its slogan, like his autobiography, was "Every Man a King."

The principles of Share Our Wealth were based on the proposals Long had been advancing in his Senate speeches since 1932. Specifically, Long advocated a capital levy tax making it impossible for a family to own more than $5 million in a lifetime and an income tax to prevent a family from earning more than $1 million in a year. From these taxes, Long hoped to provide a "homestead" of $5,000 and an annual income of $2,000 to $3,000 to every family in the United States.

Other benefits to be provided under his plan included pensions for those over 60 and financial assistance for college tuition. The government would also limit working hours in order to "prevent over-production and to give the workers of America some share in the recreations, conveniences, and luxuries of life." Finally, the government would purchase and store agricultural supplies in order to balance supply and demand and thus stabilize prices.

Long's plan was not simply a recovery scheme to end the Depression, but one that would radically alter relations within the nation's economy and create a much stronger role for the government in controlling the economy. Without providing details of the mechanics of the plan, Huey left many questions unanswered, such as how property would be assessed and shared, how the plan would be enforced, and how the money would be distributed. Huey answered the many economists who took exception to Share Our Wealth with an honest admission, "I am going to have to call in some great minds to help me."

Huey's share-the-wealth scheme was not essentially new to America. Other politicians, as well as historians and economists, had touched often on the need for a more adequate distribution of the products of labor and capital. But none had been able to dramatize it, simplify it, and popularize it as well as the Kingfish. Indeed, Huey Long was selling Share Our Wealth to Americans just the way he had sold Cottolene to Louisianians back in 1914, and just as successfully. In fact,

Castro Carazao, former orchestra leader at the Roosevelt Hotel and the band director at LSU, composed a catchy tune called "Every Man a King," that became the theme song of the organization. Its simple words evoked Long's message:

Ev'ry man a king, ev'ry man a king,
For you can be a millionaire
But there's something belonging to others.
There's enough for all people to share.

In the spring of 1934, Long supporters in Louisiana organized the first Share Our Wealth clubs. These clubs were made up of both politicians and ordinary voters who supported Long's ideas. Very quickly, fans of Huey's in other states set up their own clubs, often with help from the Share Our Wealth headquarters in Washington, D.C.

By April 1935, the Share Our Wealth office was receiving an average of 60,000 letters a week; after one radio speech, more than 30,000 letters a day poured in for 24 consecutive days. Total membership, according to the Long organization, had reached about 4 million Americans throughout the United States and included a wide range of people and organizations. Indeed, as biographer T. Harry Williams recounted, Long received support from an independent Irish-American Political Unit in Brooklyn, New York, a Foreign Bondholders National Committee in Riverdale, Maryland, and a United Mine Workers Union in Denning, Arkansas.

Not surprisingly, the appeal of Long's program to the people on the lowest rung of America's economic ladder was great: Dozens of black Share Our Wealth clubs were organized in Louisiana and in several northern states. As Huey sought to build support, he could not afford to alienate either the large numbers of black votes in the north or white voters—the only voters in his home state—who remained stubbornly racist in their attitudes. Blacks were welcome into the Share Our Wealth organization, but they could not expect Huey Long to campaign on racial matters, such as school desegregation or equal opportunities in the workplace.

"Don't say I'm working for niggers. I'm not," Long told Roy Wilkins in an article for the magazine *The Crisis*. "I'm for the poor man—all poor men. Black and white, they all gotta have a chance. They gotta have a home, a job, and a decent education for their children. 'Every Man a King'—that's my slogan. That means every man, niggers along with the rest, but not specially for niggers."

The question on everyone's lips during the spring of 1935 was: Would Huey Long run for president? Unfortunately, it did not appear likely that the Kingfish would offer a straight answer. "All this talk about my running for President is eye-wash," he told a reporter for the *Atlantic Monthly*. "I couldn't carry the states with the big electoral votes." But just a few weeks later, he told another group of journalists, "I'll tell you here and now that Franklin Roosevelt will not be the next President of the United States. If the Democrats nominate Roosevelt and the Republicans nominate Hoover, Huey Long will be your next President."

Indeed, critics all along the political spectrum in the United States saw potential danger to the United States posed by Huey Long and his plan. Liberal politicians charged that there was a tendency toward fascism in the way Long ran the government of Louisiana. Conservatives focused on the communistic nature of Huey Long's Share Our Wealth program. Both fascism and communism, as they developed in Europe, involved violent revolution, suppression of dissent, and the amassing of power in the hands of a single, all-powerful leader. They also occurred during times of economic stress, when the will of the people could be swayed by a charismatic leader—a leader, said his critics, just like Huey Long.

Huey Long denied that he was anything other than a political leader determined to carry out the will of the people. The government he ran in Louisiana was not a dictatorship of any kind, but rather a perfect democracy. "When you have a perfect democracy," he told a Washington reporter, "it is pretty hard to tell it from a dictatorship." He called Hitler, the leader of the fascist government of Germany, "that son of a bitch" and abhorred his anti-Semitism. "Anybody that lets his public policies be mixed up with religious prejudice," Huey stated, "is a plain Goddamned fool." He reacted with equal vigor at being called a communist. "This plan is the only defense this country's got against communism," claiming that if the wealthy in this country did not willingly share with those in need, the poor would rise up and take power and resources just as they had in Russia in 1917.

Whatever historians and politicians labeled Huey Long, millions of people across the country were being drawn to his message. Clearly, the Roosevelt administration had to prepare itself for the challenge Long could present in the 1936 election. In early 1935, James Farley and Harold Ickes, two prominent members of the administration, took a secret poll of Huey Long's national strength.

Interviewing more than 21,000 members of the 1932 electorate, they determined that Huey could expect to gather at least 2.7 million votes and as many as 4 million running on a third-party ticket. They also estimated that he would garner 222 votes in the electoral college. Although it appeared unlikely that Huey could win the election, he remained a significant threat: In several states, he would divert enough votes away from Roosevelt to allow the Republican candidate, whoever it might be, to win.

In the summer of 1935, Roosevelt unveiled a potent weapon against Huey Long: new federal legislation to fight the Great Depression. Telling one of his aides he intended to "steal Long's thunder," President Roosevelt introduced, and the legislature passed, the highest income, inheritance, and gift tax bill in the nation's history, a Social Security act to provide income for the elderly, and the largest public works program ever to be launched on a national basis. Although many of these programs had been under consideration for some time, there is no doubt that the timing of their passage was calculated to undermine Long's spreading appeal.

The New York *World Telegram* captured the tactic succinctly in one of its stories, "With one quick jab, [Roosevelt] seemed to puncture Huey Long's share the wealth balloon and rob the Louisiana Senator of his chief issue." Will Rogers, the Oklahoma-born folk philosopher, commented on the move in one of his newspaper columns: "I would sure like to have seen Huey's face when he was woke up in the middle of the night by the President, who said, 'Lay over, Huey, I want to get in bed with you.'"

Nevertheless, Huey Long opposed most of the second New Deal legislation as vigorously as he had opposed the first, and for largely the same reasons: Roosevelt's measures did not go far enough to fundamentally alter the economic structure of the United States. In fact, his remarks about the various bills that came before him take up more room in the 1935 *Congressional Record* than any three other members of the Senate combined. His filibusters, long speeches meant to delay the passage of bills, continued to annoy his colleagues but thrill the visitors who lined up to see the Kingfish in action. One of his filibusters lasted 15½ hours without a break.

Now fully aware of the danger it faced from the "Terror of the Bayous," the Roosevelt administration increased its campaign to undermine Huey Long's power and appeal, a campaign that it had waged, often subtly and secretly, almost since the day Roosevelt entered the White House. In fact, a powerful, if informal, alliance between the Roosevelt administration and anti-Long forces in Louisiana had been formed as early as 1932.

Using a combination of techniques—techniques they labeled unscrupulous when Huey Long used them—the state government and federal government slowly but steadily attempted to undermine Huey Long's power. First, a series of hearings, instigated by anti-Long forces in Louisiana and conducted by a Senate subcommittee, publicized the unethical practices of the Long organization in Louisiana in 1932. Long's "deduct system," his hiring and firing methods, and the campaign practices of his supporters came under public scrutiny.

For months, Louisiana's political dirty laundry was hung out to dry in front of the American people. Perhaps most painful to Huey was the fact that two of his brothers, Earl and Julius, testified against him. Julius also gave a series of interviews, published in local newspapers and reprinted in the national magazine *Real America,* condemning his brother and the Long machine. "There has never been such an administration of ego and pomposity since the days of Nero," Julius stated.

Although no criminal charges were brought, the hearings sparked an investigation by the U.S. Treasury Department into the Long organization's finances. Claiming that Huey Long and his associates were embezzling from the state government and not paying income tax on the money they stole, anti-Longs were more than happy to provide testimony to federal agents. In 1934, the investigation culminated with the arrest and conviction of several of Huey's associates for income tax evasion.

Roosevelt's most damaging weapon against Huey Long in his home state involved the dispersement of federal patronage in the state. Starting in the fall of 1933, nearly every Internal Revenue Service agent, federal judge, federal attorney, and federal marshal appointed or elected during this period was overtly anti-Long in his politics. Every job created through New Deal legislation, which numbered in the thousands, were also granted to those who opposed the Long machine.

In fact, it appeared that being against Huey Long was the only requirement needed to receive a federal job in the state. Long, with some justification, would complain to reporters in 1935 that the Roosevelt administration was rewarding the "most rebuked, repudiated, consciousless characters known to enter the public or the private life of Louisiana or any other state."

Part of the reason for the successs of Long's enemies in Louisiana was the fact that the Great Depression continued to hold the state in its grip. The poor of Louisiana grew poorer every day and the Kingfish who had promised so much seemed unable and, his enemies would say, unwilling, to help them. Although his public works programs continued, free school-books and paved roads no longer impressed those who needed food in their bellies and a roof over their heads.

More than 15% of Louisiana citizens were on public relief in 1933, and they received help not from Huey Long, but from the New Deal programs enacted by the federal government the previous spring—the very same programs the Kingfish had relentlessly attacked. In this Southern state, loyalty to the Democratic Party had been a way of life since the Civil War. By opposing Roosevelt and other members of the party, Huey Long had committed an egregious political act. His enemies would make the most of it.

Ironically, anti-Long forces, among the most economically and politically conservative men in the country, would gain power and influence by courting Franklin Delano Roosevelt, who had introduced some of the most progressive legislation in United States history. Although the New Deal did not go far enough for Huey Long, it had dramatically increased the responsibility of the government for the welfare of its people—the very principle the Bourbon Democrats had refused to accept throughout their reign. That reign had ended when Huey Long arrived in the governor's office in 1928 and Roosevelt in the White House in 1932.

The erosion of Long's influence in the state deepened with each passing month, and became increasingly tinged with the threat of violence. "At that time, there were men all over the state who believed that Huey had to be killed, that to kill him would be a moral act," admitted A. M. Wallace, an anti-Long leader of a north Louisiana parish. J. Y. Sanders, ex-governor of Louisiana and one of Huey's most bitter enemies, spoke of revolution in speeches across the state. "We do not have to wait for any election," he told a crowd in Donaldson, Louisiana.

Huey Long was down, but he was not out. He clamped down on dissent throughout the state, punishing his opponents more harshly and amassing more control over state politics than ever before. From November 1934 to August 1935, Huey Long called five special sessions of the state legislature. In the eight-day November session alone, a total of 44 bills were passed, thanks in large part to the ubiquitous presence of the Kingfish himself. Although state law prohibited it, Long appeared in the chambers of the legislature to encourage, cajole, and threaten. "I can frighten or buy ninety-nine out of one hundred men," Long admitted, and he proved it by seeing every one of his bills passed.

During this period, Long introduced a number of progressive bills, including the abolition of the poll tax. For the first time in at least 50 years, Louisiana citizens could register without having to pay for the right to vote. Long also levied Louisiana's first income tax, which exempted the poor and imposed a 6% tax on incomes over $50,000. In the spring of 1935, his Debt Moratorium Act suspended all debts, except those owed to the government, for two years.

These measures, and others, helped Huey shore up support among his most loyal supporters, the poor people of Louisiana. How effective they were in doing so, however, is difficult to calculate, for Huey Long took no chances when it came to future elections. "I'm always afraid of an election," he told state senator Harry Gilbert, "you can't tell what will happen." A law introduced in April 1935 took away the right of local parishes to appoint election commissioners and poll watchers and gave it to the governor.

In fact, most of the bills Huey introduced in 1934 and 1935 were designed to consign all political and economic power in the state to the governor's office. He enhanced the powers of the Bureau of Criminal Identification, an agency made up of plainclothes state police, which essentially created a state militia completely under his domain; soon, all police and fire departments throughout the state would also be monitored in this way. In order to quell criticism from the press, Long imposed a tax on all newspapers in Louisiana with circulations of more than 20,000. Ostensibly meant to raise revenue, Huey Long admitted that he designed the tax to be a "tax on lying, two cents per lie."

Tension continued to mount throughout the state. In January 1935, Huey Long was forced to declare martial law in East Baton Rouge parish when a paramilitary organization, formed by ex-governors Parker and Pleasant and Major Walmsey of New Orleans, took over the parish courthouse. Although violence was averted, and troops were removed within a few weeks, martial law officially continued in the state capital for over six months.

Huey Long could no longer control his state by the force of his personality and his growing number of opponents knew it. Rumors of assassination plots against the Kingfish, always present, flourished during the spring and summer of 1935. In August, Huey announced on the Senate floor that a group of his enemies had met in a New Orleans hotel, called the De Soto, to plan his death. At this meeting, in which Long claimed to have planted spies, five men discussed the plan in depth. "I haven't the slightest doubt," said one of the plotters, "but that Roosevelt would pardon anyone who killed Long."

Although Huey Long had feared assassination during much of his public life, he had a strong premonition during this period that his days were numbered. On August 26, 1935, shortly before he left Washington for Louisiana, he told a colleague, "I may not be back here. This may be my swan song for all I know." And to state senator Harry Byrd, Huey frankly admitted, "Harry, those people are going to kill me. There is no way in the world I can keep those people from killing me."

Nevertheless, Huey Long arrived in Baton Rouge on the morning of September 8, 1935, prepared to do to do battle once again.

10

THE DEATH AND AFTERLIFE OF HUEY LONG

"God, don't let me die, I have so much to do."

—*Huey P. Long*

Since the moment the fatal bullet was fired, controversy has raged over the Long assassination. Immediately following the incident, rumors spread like wildfire that the assassin, Dr. Carl Weiss, had been part of a larger conspiracy to kill the Kingfish, that he had been at the De Soto Hotel meeting earlier in the summer, and that he had been hired by anti-Longs inside and outside Louisiana. Another theory held that Weiss was not guilty at all, and that Huey's own bodyguards had killed their leader, either by accident or design.

The answer to the mystery of who shot Huey Long and why may never be answered fully to everyone's satisfaction. To date, however, no proof has been offered to refute the conclusion that Carl Weiss fired the fatal shot and that he acted alone. As recently as 1992, a report issued by the State of Louisiana Department of Public Safety and Corrections concluded that Dr. Weiss was responsible for Huey Long's death.

Following the assassination, the remains of Huey Long lay in state in the capitol rotunda for two days as more than 80,000 mourners filed by his casket. The mood in the capital was a mixture of shock, sadness, and resignation. "There was a feeling of relief, even among his own people," a House member recalled. "I can't begin to get over to you the tension that had been gripping the state."

On Thursday, September 12, 1935, about 175,000 people from all over the state and across the country arrived to pay

Approximately 175,000 people from all over Louisiana and across the country flocked to Baton Rouge to bid farewell to the fallen Kingfish. (Louisiana State Library)

their last respects to the fallen Kingfish. His enemies attended as well as his friends, some of them "just to make sure he was dead." Huey Long's sealed casket was carried down the 48 granite steps toward a grave that had been dug in the sunken garden facing his greatest public works project, the new state capitol building. Later, a monument would be placed at the grave site with the inscription: "Here lies Louisiana's great son Huey Pierce Long, an unconquered friend of the poor who dreamed of the day when the wealth of the land would be spread among the people." As the crowd departed at the end of the burial ceremony, the LSU band played "Every Man A King" in slow time.

Long's death made headlines across the country. Most press coverage was unfavorable, as it had been throughout the Kingfish's tumultuous career. Long's obituary published in the New York *Daily News* on September 11, for instance, read in part: "Huey Long was a political genius and an evil one. We have to discuss him in the political aspect and in his political aspect we can find nothing good to say about him." The New York *Times* wrote, "If Fascism ever comes in the United States, it will come in something that way . . . The danger is, as Senator Long demonstrated in Louisiana, that freedom may be done away with in the name of efficiency and a strong paternal government."

Huey Long did indeed subvert the democratic process in order to reach his goals: His unorthodox methods of campaigning and raising revenue, his iron-fisted control over the legislature and the men who served in it, and his manipulation of the law could not, and still cannot, be excused as "politics as usual." However, charges of fascism are spurious unless also applied to the Bourbon Democrats before him—politicians who had far less worthy goals in mind when they used the same tools of corruption to remain in power for decades.

As a blunt and unequivocal spokesman for the common man, Huey Long was a compelling figure on the national political stage during the final years of his life. His pressure on Roosevelt to bring more fundamental changes to the country's economic structure—in essence to give the poor and working man a greater share of resources—certainly influenced the construction of the second New Deal. And, without doubt, his growing popularity with men and women across the country challenged the Roosevelt administration as did that of no other candidate.

Indeed, Long's assassination, coming as it did before the campaign of 1936 got underway, considerably relieved Roosevelt's burden. As one astute Louisiana citizen told a reporter at the time, "On your way home, ask Senator Joe Robinson of Arkansas. Ask Pat Harrison of Mississippi. Ask almost any senator. To a lot of those gents, the murder of Huey Long must have been like lifting the mortgage on the old homestead. Ask President Roosevelt."

Following Huey's assassination, the pressure on the Roosevelt reelection campaign posed by the Share Our Wealth organization eased almost immediately. Without a charismatic leader willing to fight Roosevelt on the national stage and with the increasing success of the New Deal programs being felt throughout the country, the Share Our Wealth organization slowly but steadily lost momentum. Roosevelt easily won reelection in 1936.

Long's influence in Louisiana, however, was deep and long-lasting. Soon after his death, a ticket made up of pro-Long politicians was swept into office, including Earl Long as lieutenant governor. For a time, it seemed as if Huey Long's plans for Louisiana had been granted a new lease on life. Just a few months before his death, however, Huey Long had made a prediction: "If I don't live long enough to undo the centralization of government I've built up in this state, all these men around me are going to end up in the penitentiary. I can't keep 'em from stealing now."

Unfortunately for Louisiana, it was a remarkably accurate prediction: For the next four years or so, the men who had taken up the Long banner, with the possible exception of Earl Long himself, shamelessly pillaged the state. "When I took the oath as Governor," admitted Richard Leche, "I didn't take any vows of poverty." In 1936, Leche admitted that he earned over $90,000 during his first year as governor, despite the fact that the official governor's salary was just $7,500. James Monroe Smith, the president of LSU, embezzled more than $500,000 of university funds in little more than three years. Huey's "deduct" system rose to new heights of audacity, raking in nearly $100 million during the same period.

In 1939, the state that had long been known for its tolerant attitude toward corruption launched a series of investigations into the Long machine. Within months, the ranking members of the Long organization were in jail or on their way, including Governor Leche (who resigned in disgrace, leaving Earl Long to take over as governor), James Smith, and Huey's old friend Seymour Weiss.

Until 1948, the people of Louisiana elected candidates who promised to clean up the government and yet still provide the benefits that Huey Long had brought to them. None were able to do so. In 1948, they returned their loyalty to the Long family, sending Huey's brother Earl to the governor's office with a landslide victory. For nearly 40 years thereafter, the Long family name would be found on political office doors in both Louisiana and Washington.

Earl himself served a successful four-year gubernatorial term starting in 1948; he won again in 1956 when he was next eligible to take office. Twenty-five years after Huey's death, the sentiments the Kingfish had espoused were uttered once again by his younger brother. "We got the finest roads, finest hospitals, finest schools in the country," Earl told a crowd in Baton Rouge, "yet there are rich men who complain. They are so tight you can hear 'em squeak when they walk."

Finding away around the Louisiana rule that no governor could succeed himself by resigning from office a few weeks before his second official term ended, Earl won reelection for the third time in 1960. His victory was all the more astounding to outside observers when the tumultuous events of the campaign were considered: On June 26, 1959, in the midst of the campaign, Earl Long had been committed to the state institution for the mentally ill at Mandeville; his erratic behavior, including his very public relationship with a New Orleans stripper, had caused friends and family to institutionalize him. Nevertheless, Earl Long apparently engendered the same kind of support in the voters of Louisiana as had Huey. He died, however, before he could take office.

In the meantime, Huey's son Russell had been elected to the United States Senate in 1950 to begin what would be a 37-year tenure. As chairman of the powerful Senate Finance Committee, Russell attempted to simplify the tax code and place a heavier tax burden on the wealthy. George Long, Huey and Earl's next older brother, went to Congress as a Louisiana representative in 1952. Two younger Long cousins, then the widow of one, held the same congressional seat from 1963 through 1986. In general, Huey's political family members tended to espouse similar social ideas and, in varying degrees, attracted the same warm and loyal support from their constituents that Huey had enjoyed throughout much of his career.

How much Huey Long, and the Long family members who followed him in politics, helped the average Louisiana citizen on a practical level remains a matter of much debate. Without question, Huey's programs to build roads and bridges and improve education did much to alleviate the suffering of the poor during his tenure. He did not, however, incorporate his programs into stable, lasting agents of change. In many ways, as biographer Glen Jeansonn put it, Huey "changed the style of state politics more than its substance." Even today, Louisiana ranks among the lowest states in terms of per capita income and literacy and among the highest in crime, poverty, and infant mortality.

Nevertheless, what Huey Long did bring into state and national politics was the voice and concerns of the common man. Through his words and his actions, he pushed forward the poor and working man's struggle for an equal chance at the American dream. In that sense, he followed in the Populist tradition that had once flourished in his hometown of Winn in north Louisiana. Had Huey Long not lived at a time and place in which racism so completely stained the fabric of political life, he might have been able to forge the alliance between black and white that had eluded the Populists of 1890 and that had so terrified the Bourbon Democrats. His national Share Our Wealth organization, with its outreach to blacks across the country, might have succeeded in doing just that.

The people who mattered most to Huey Long, and who loved him most, summed up his legacy perhaps better than any historian or journalist. "At least we got *something*," a North Louisiana farmer said. "Before him, we got nothing. That's the difference."

BIBLIOGRAPHY

PRIMARY SOURCES

The Interview Collection in T. Harry Williams Papers, located in the Louisiana and Lower Mississippi Valley Collections, Hill Memorial Library, Louisiana State University at Baton Rouge remains the most essential source of information about Huey Long's life. Williams interviewed 298 people who had known, worked with, supported, or fought against the Kingfish. Although the transcripts of the interviews are often edited, the documents are lively and informative.

The Conway Collection, seven large scrapbooks of newspaper clippings and political pamphlets, follows Long's career from 1928 until his death in 1935. It is located in the State Library at Baton Rouge and available through interlibrary loan.

Another interesting source of information, especially about Huey Long's youth, are the Harley B. Bozeman Scrapbooks, a collection of articles originally printed in a Winnfield, Louisiana. Between 1957 and 1969, Bozeman, who had been Long's closest friend until politics divided them in 1929, reminisced about their friendship and about Huey's life. Considering the bitter end to their relationship, the pieces are remarkably balanced and entertaining.

Copies of Long's own newspaper, the *Louisiana Progress* (called the *American Progress* after 1933), are available at the Hill Memorial Library at Louisiana State University at Baton Rouge. They convey Huey's slant on his own career and on political life in Louisiana and the United States better than any biography or even his own autobiography ever could. Other newspaper coverage of his career—equally biased—can be found in the Baton Rouge *Morning Advocate,* the New Orleans *Times-Picayune,* and the New Orleans *States* and the *Item;* most of these newspapers were strongly anti-Long throughout much of the Kingfish's career. The New York *Times* was a terrific source of information about Huey Long's national career as was the Washington *Post*.

Of course, the most valuable primary source of information about the Kingfish is his own autobiography, *Every Man a King: The Autobiography of Huey P. Long* (New Orleans, 1933), a highly readable, if self-serving, account of his life. Another attempt at revealing something of his personal life was *My First Days in the White House* (Harrisburg, Pa.: Telegraph Press, 1935), a book that Huey planned to release to promote his bid for the presidency; it was published shortly after his death. This book portrayed what the world would be like when Huey Long became president of the United States—happy, economically sound, and with the corporate bigwigs he had fought against in subservient positions.

BIOGRAPHIES

Huey Long has been the subject of more than a dozen biographies. Perhaps the most famous is not a biography at all, but rather a novel called *All the King's Men* by Robert Penn Warren (New York: Harcourt Brace, 1946); although it is hardly accurate in detail, it does provide a dramatic introduction to the life and times of Huey Long.

The three biographies published before Long's death are also the most partisan: John Kingston Fineran's *The Career of a Tinpot Napolean* (published by the author, New Orleans, 1933), is particularly virulent and contains many factual errors; Forrest Davis' *Huey Long: A Candid Biography* (New York: Dodge Publishing Co., 1935); and Carleton Beals' *The Story of Huey P. Long* (Philadelphia: J. B. Lippincott Co., 1935). Beals recognized Huey's methods and compared them to those of a Latin American dictator, but also allowed that the Bourbons themselves were ruthless. Thomas O. Harris, another contemporary journalist who opposed the Long administration, published *The Kingfish: Huey P. Long, Dictator* (New Orleans: Pelican Publishing Company, 1938) a few years after Long's death. Well written and relatively accurate, Harris' biography is nonetheless colored by his rather hostile relationship with his subject.

Of the modern biographies, *Huey Long* by T. Harry Williams (New York: Alfred A. Knopf, 1969) is considered the most comprehensive and accurate. It is also the most benevolent, casting Huey Long as a mass leader whose excesses were excusable within the political and historical context of his times. A major flaw with this book is its length and the extent of its detail; only someone with a deep and abiding interest in Huey Long would find it necessary to read nearly 900 pages about him. William Ivy Hair's *The Kingfish and His Realm: The Life and Times of Huey Long* (Baton Rouge: Louisiana State University Press, 1991) is an extremely accessible, well-written book that places Huey Long's story within the setting of race and class in Louisiana. *Messiah of the Masses* by Glen Jeansonne (New York: HarperCollins, 1993) is a fast-paced, highly critical examination of Huey Long's life written for the college student.

An interesting compendium of articles by and about Huey Long is *Huey P. Long: Southern Demagogue or American Democrat,* edited by Henry C. Dethloff (Lafayette, Louisiana: The University of Southern Louisiana, 1976). Excerpts from Long's speeches and pamphlets are reproduced as are excerpts from longer biographical works on Long by such historians as Arthur Schlesinger, T. Harry Williams, and Allan P. Sindler.

Several books have been written about Huey Long's assassination and the controversy that continues to surround it. The most well-known, and one that has been recently updated with new information, is David Zinman's *The Day Huey Long Was Shot* (New York: Ivan Obolensky, Inc., 1982). A must for conspiracy buffs, this book includes interviews with the assassin's family, as well as comments by Russell Long, Huey's son, who was just 14 when his father was killed.

Huey's equally intriguing younger brother Earl is the subject of at least two well-known and very readable biographies, the insightful and often hilarious *The Earl of Louisiana* by A. J. Liebling and *Earl K. Long: The Sage of Uncle Earl and Louisiana Politics* by Michael L. Kurtz and Morgan D. Peoples (Baton Rouge: Louisiana State University Press, 1990), which sheds valuable light on Earl's life and his political contributions to the state of Louisiana after Huey's death.

LOUISIANA AND GENERAL HISTORY

Understanding the history of Louisiana, and of the South in general, is essential if one is to appreciate the life of Huey Long and his impact on American politics. I found *Louisiana: A History* by Bennett H. Wall, Light Townsend Cummins, Joe Gray Taylor, William Ivy Hair, Mark T. Carleton, and Michael Kurtz (Arlington Heights, Ill.: Forum Press, 1990) to be an excellent, easy-to-read introduction to the state. William Ivy Hair's *Bourbonism and Agrarian Protest: Louisiana Politics 1877–1900* (Baton Rouge: Louisiana State University Press, 1969) and Roger W. Shugg's *Origins of Class Struggle in Louisiana* examine the Bourbon era in Louisiana during which Huey Long, and his political perspective, developed.

Important books that place Huey Long within the context of the Great Depression and the politics engendered by this national crisis include: *The Politics of Upheaval* by Arthur M. Schlesinger, Jr. (Boston: Houghton Mifflin Company, 1960); *American Messiahs* by Franklin Carter Hope (New York: Simon and Schuster, 1935); Raymond Graham Swing's *Forerunners of American Fascism* (New York: Julian Messner, 1935); and Alan Brinkley's *Voices of Protest: Huey Long, Father Coughlin, and the Great Depression* (New York: Alfred A. Knopf, 1982).

INDEX

Boldface page numbers indicate main topics
Italic page numbers indicate illustrations.